LifeLight

"In Him was life, and that life was the light of men." John 1:4

Revelation

LEADERS GUIDE

I0806857

CONCORDIA PUBLISHING HOUSE · SAINT LOUIS

Through dramatic symbolism, Revelation shows the spiritual conflict that surrounds life in this sinful world. At the center stands Christ, the Lamb of God slain for sinners. With the heavenly Father's blessing, Christ triumphs over Satan and opens for you the paradise of heaven, the city of God.

3558 S. Jefferson Ave., St. Louis, MO 63118-3968.
1-800-325-304 • cph.org

Revised from material prepared by Edward G. Kettner and Walter W. Stuenkel.

Earl H. Gaulke, editor

Denise Muhly and Lavern Schmidt, field-test coordinators

LifeLight field-test site: St. Peter Lutheran Church, Lodi, California

Developed under the auspices of the LifeLight Committee of The Lutheran Church—Missouri Synod, with funding assistance from the International Lutheran Women's Missionary League.

Quotations marked KJV are from the King James or Authorized Version of the Bible.

This publication may be available in Braille, in large print, or on cassette tape for the visually impaired. Please allow 8 to 12 weeks for delivery. Write to Lutheran Braille Workers, P.O. Box 5000, Yucaipa, CA 92399; call toll-free 1-800-925-6092; or visit the Web site: www.LBWinc.org.

Manufactured in the U.S.A.

Cover illustration: © Richard Heroldt

7 8 9 10 11 12 13 29 28 27 26 25 24 23 22

Contents

Introduction

Welcome to LifeLight

A special pleasure is in store for you. You will be instrumental in leading your brothers and sisters in Christ closer to Him who is our life and light (John 1:4). You will have the pleasure of seeing fellow Christians discover new insights and rediscover old ones as they open the Scriptures and dig deep into them, perhaps deeper than they have ever dug before. More than that, you will have the pleasure of sharing in this wonderful study.

LifeLight—An In-depth Study

LifeLight is a series of in-depth Bible studies. The goal of LifeLight is that through a regular program of in-depth personal and group study of Scripture, more and more Christian adults may grow in their personal faith in Jesus Christ, enjoy fellowship with the members of His body, and reach out in love to others in witness and service.

In-depth means that this Bible study includes the following four components: individual daily home study; discussion in a small group; a lecture presentation on the Scripture portion under study; and an enhancement of the week's material (through reading the enrichment magazine).

LifeLight Participants

LifeLight participants are adults who desire a deeper study of the Scriptures than is available in the typical Sunday morning adult Bible class. (Mid-to-older teens might also be LifeLight participants.) While LifeLight does not assume an existing knowledge of the Bible or special experience or skills in Bible study, it does assume a level of commitment that will bring participants to each of the nine weekly assemblies having read the assigned readings and attempted to answer the study questions. Daily reading and study will require from 15 to 30 minutes for the five days preceding the LifeLight assembly. The day following the assembly will be spent reviewing the previous week's study by going over the completed study leaflet and the enrichment magazine.

LifeLight Leadership

While the in-depth process used by LifeLight begins with individual study and cannot achieve its aims without this individual effort, it cannot be completed by individual study alone. Therefore, trained leaders are necessary. You fill one or perhaps more of the important roles described below.

The Director

This person oversees the LifeLight program in a local center (which may be a congregation or a center operated by several neighboring congregations). The director

- serves as the parish LifeLight overall coordinator and leader;
- coordinates the scheduling of the LifeLight program;
- orders materials;
- convenes LifeLight leadership team meetings;
- develops publicity materials;
- recruits participants;
- maintains records and budgeting;
- assigns, with the leadership team, participants to small discussion groups;
- makes arrangements for facilities;
- communicates outreach opportunities to small-group leaders and to congregational boards;
- follows up on participants who leave the program.

The Assistant Director *(optional)*

This person may assist the director. Duties listed for the director may be assigned to the assistant director as mutually agreeable.

The Lecture Leader

This person prepares and delivers the lecture at the weekly assembly. **(Lesson material for the lecture leader begins on p. 9.)** The lecture leader

- prepares and presents the Bible study lecture to the large group;
- prepares worship activities (devotional thought, hymn, prayer), using resources in the study leaflet and leaders guide and possibly other outside sources;
- helps the small-group discussion leaders to grow in understanding the content of the lessons;
- encourages prayer at weekly leadership-team and discussion-leaders meetings.

The Small-Group Coordinator *(optional; the director may fill this role)*

This person supervises and coordinates the work of the small-group discussion leaders. The small-group coordinator

- recruits with the leadership team the small-group discussion leaders;
- trains or arranges for training of the discussion leaders;
- assists the director and discussion leaders in follow-up and outreach;
- encourages the discussion leaders to contact absent group members;
- participates in the weekly leadership-team and discussion-leaders equipping meetings;
- provides ongoing training and support as needed.

The Small-Group Discussion Leaders

These people guide and facilitate discussion of LifeLight participants in the small groups. **(Lesson material for the small-group leaders begins on p. 56.)** There should be one discussion leader for every group of no more than 12 participants. The small-group discussion leaders are, perhaps, those individuals who are most important to the success of the program. They should, therefore, be chosen with special care and be equipped with skills needed to guide discussion and to foster a caring fellowship within the group. These discussion leaders

- prepare each week for the small-group discussion by using the study leaflet and small-group leaders guide section for that session **(see p. 56)**;
- read the enrichment magazine as a study supplement;
- guide and facilitate discussion in their small group;
- encourage and assist the discussion group in prayer;
- foster fellowship and mutual care within the discussion group;
- attend weekly discussion-leaders training meetings.

Leadership Training

LifeLight leaders will meet weekly to review the previous week's work and plan the coming week. At this session, leaders can address concerns and prepare for the coming session. LifeLight is a 1½-hour program with no possibility for it to be taught in the one hour typically available on Sunday mornings. Some congregations, however, may want to use the Sunday morning Bible study hour for LifeLight preparation and leadership training. In such a meeting, the lecture leader and/or small-group coordinator may lead the discussion leaders through the coming week's lesson, reserving 5 or 10 minutes for problem solving or other group concerns.

While it requires intense effort, LifeLight has proven to bring great benefit to LifeLight participants. The effort put into this program, both by leaders and by participants, will be rewarding and profitable.

The LifeLight Weekly Schedule

Here is how LifeLight will work week by week:

1. Before session 1, each participant will receive the study leaflet for session 1 and the enrichment magazine for the course. The study leaflet contains worship resources (for use both in individual daily study and at the opening of the following week's assembly) and readings and study questions for five days. Challenge questions will lead those participants who have the time and desire a greater challenge into even deeper levels of study.
2. After the five days of individual study at home, participants will gather for a weekly assembly of all LifeLight participants. The assembly will begin with a brief period of worship (5 minutes). Participants will then join their assigned small discussion groups (of 12 or fewer, who will remain the same throughout the course), where they will go over the week's study questions together (55 minutes). Assembling

together once again, participants will listen to a lecture presentation on the readings they have studied in the previous week and discussed in their small groups (20 minutes). After the lecture presentation, the director or another leader will distribute the study leaflet for the following week. Closing announcements and other necessary business may take another five minutes before dismissal.

In some places some small groups will not join the weekly assembly because of scheduling or other reasons. Such groups may meet at another time and place (perhaps in the home of one of the small group's members). A congregation may record the lecture given by the lecture leader at the weekly assembly and duplicate it for use by other groups meeting later in the week.

3. On the day following the assembly, participants will review the preceding week's work by rereading the study leaflet they completed (and that they perhaps supplemented or corrected during the discussion in their small group) and by reading appropriate articles in the enrichment magazine.

Then the LifeLight weekly study process will begin all over again!

Recommended Study Resources for Revelation

Brighton, Louis A. *Revelation* (Concordia Commentary Series). St. Louis: Concordia Publishing House, 1999. The author sees Ascension Christology as the heart of the prophetic message, and he relates the imagery to the church's life and worship. A thorough exposition by a well-known professor, scholar, and expert on the book.

The Lutheran Study Bible. St. Louis: Concordia Publishing House, 2009. This resource contains more than 26,000 study and application notes, a most thorough reference guide (pp. lxv–cx), and over 90,000 cross-references, as well as a 31,000-entry concordance, maps, charts, and timelines.

Reformation Heritage Bible Commentary: Revelation. St. Louis: Concordia Publishing House, 2012. This new Bible commentary series is a powerful tool for those wanting to better understand the background information on authorship, history, settings, and themes of the Gospel. Features the ESV and KJV side by side with quotes from key reformers.

Franzmann, Martin H. *The Revelation to John*. A Commentary. St. Louis: Concordia Publishing House, 1968. Scholarly yet popularly written exposition.

Lenski, R. C. H. *The Interpretation of St. John's Revelation*. Minneapolis: Augsburg Publishing House, 1963. A resource concerned with faithfully expounding the true message of Revelation.

Roehrs, Walter R., and Martin H. Franzmann. *Concordia Self-Study Commentary*. St. Louis: Concordia Publishing House, 1979. An invaluable one-volume commentary on the Bible.

The Concordia Organist is a 31-CD collection of pipe organ accompaniments for all the hymns and liturgical music in *Lutheran Service Book*. St. Louis: Concordia Publishing House (order no. 99-2264). Use these CDs for worship hymn accompaniment.

Understanding the Book of Revelation

Revelation 1:1–8

Preparing for the Session

Central Focus

To more fully understand this last book of the New Testament and to derive the full comfort and inspiration it can give to dedicated Bible students, it is necessary to recognize the centrality of Jesus Christ as the risen Savior and victorious Lord in the midst of all the problems and persecutions of the early Christians. To gain this understanding, Bible students must be alert to such features of Revelation as apocalyptic writing, frequent Old Testament allusions, and the church-historical approach in interpretation.

Objectives

That participants, led by the Holy Spirit, will

1. gain appreciation of the nature and purpose of apocalyptic writing and its fitting use, considering the historical situation prevailing in the early Christian church;
2. develop a richer understanding and deeper trust in Jesus Christ as the victorious Lord through the varied inspired apocalyptic symbols and pictures; and
3. acquire greater courage and skill to express personal Christian hope more effectively to those enduring trials and tribulations today.

Note for the small-group leaders: Lesson notes and other materials you will need begin on page 56.

For the Director

Through Bible teaching, study, and discussion, the Holy Spirit works to nurture Christian faith and life—even under the most adverse circumstances. What a thrill and a joy to be used by Him as a LifeLight leader! As director, you have great responsibility in the physical setup for the class sessions. Develop a checklist to provide, as far as possible, the ideal setting for every participant, but especially for the presenter.

Here are some questions for the checklist: Are all the places cleared that will be necessary for all the classes? Are these places clean and comfortable and inviting? Are they ventilated properly? Is necessary equipment (chairs, tables, chalkboard, chalk, podium or lectern, overhead projector and screen) available? Is the room labeled precisely for each class? Are sheets of paper and pens and pencils provided for those desiring to take notes?

For students properly to fit themselves in the geographic setting of the Book of Revelation, it will be practically necessary for you to supply a map of the Mediterranean world. In the very first session, students should learn the location of Jerusalem, Rome, Patmos, and the seven cities of Asia Minor emphasized in the first three chapters of the Book of Revelation.

For the Lecture Leader

We can well imagine that many lay leaders, men and women, will shy away from being presenters in a study of the Book of Revelation. Even pastors and professional teachers may be reluctant to serve in this capacity because of the strangeness of apocalyptic writing.

You have consented to be a presenter, and we pray God's blessing upon your effort. It can be a wonderful Christian experience. Here are a few suggestions:

1. Spend much time in prayer, both before and after each presentation. Ask the Holy Spirit to open your understanding and to guide your study that you may truly receive what He offers you through His Word.

2. Then approach your study of the Word with eager expectancy. Always remember Paul's inspired word to Timothy: "Do your best to present yourself to God as one approved, a worker who has no need to be ashamed, rightly handling the word of truth" (2 Timothy 2:15). Remember, the Word has inherent power not only to do great things *through* you but also *for* you.

3. Preferably read the entire section of the presentation for a given week through completely at the beginning of your preparation. Then review it in your mind to see if you have grasped the thrust of it. How does it fit

to the previous material? Are there any new terms or concepts to define? Do you see how the objectives will be met? Can you freely present the biblical material in your own words? Do you see Jesus in it as the victorious Lord and Savior?

Session Plan

Worship

Begin the first LifeLight assembly with a hearty welcome to the participants. Immediately develop an atmosphere of promptness. Start the first session at the established time. Be cheerful and cordial in your demeanor and expression. Normally, the devotional period should be limited to five minutes.

Introduce the worship by telling the participants that this series of Bible studies will emphasize that "through many tribulations we must enter the kingdom of God" (Acts 14:22), but these hardships will all be truly worthwhile because we are assured that in due time we will receive eternal joy and glory in heaven through the victory of our Lord Jesus Christ.

Begin the session with the hymn printed in the study leaflet. Accompaniments are available in denominational hymnals, such as *Lutheran Service Book* or *Lutheran Worship* (refer to hymnal index). (Note: Concordia Publishing House has available *The Concordia Organist*. All the initial worship hymns in the LifeLight courses are included in this resource. It's especially helpful for mission congregations and small parishes. See the list of study resources on page 7.)

Join together in the prayer printed in the study leaflet.

Lecture Presentation

Introduction

The Book of Revelation holds great fascination for Christians and has done so ever since it was written. As we see the uncertainty that exists in the world around us, it is natural to wonder what the future holds. Since the opening verse of the book declares that God gave this revelation to John "to show to His servants the things that must soon take place" (Revelation 1:1), many people throughout the history of the church have carefully scrutinized the book in an effort to find specific predictions of today's events in the events announced in the visions. That is still going on today. Inevitably, they are disappointed, for they fail to see that the real purpose of the book is to give comfort to Christians at all times. When God's people fear that the world is raging out of control, they see here that God is always in control of history.

1 Apocalyptic Literature

As we begin a look at Revelation, we need to be prepared for a Bible study that will be quite different from any other New Testament study we might undertake. The book is written in a style that is quite different from the other books of the New Testament, a style known as *apocalyptic*.

Apocalyptic writings seem strange to us, because they are in a literary form that is quite different from anything we have today. However, the form was not unknown at the time this book was written. During the years surrounding the coming of Christ, while the Jewish nation was struggling under foreign domination, apocalyptic writing came into being. Quite often, these works were ascribed to major biblical characters who supposedly predicted the future and described the destiny of the world and of humanity.

In spite of the fact that most of this literature was not written by the men to whom they are ascribed (scholars call these works *Pseudepigrapha*, meaning "false writings"), God Himself from time to time inspired His prophets to write using this type of literature. Apocalyptic writing occurs in the books of Ezekiel, Daniel, and Zechariah in the Old Testament.

Since apocalyptic writings had been used to bring great comfort during times of trouble and persecution. Jewish readers particularly would have recognized the Book of Revelation for what it is—a book of encouragement in time of trouble, when the temptation to fall away from the faith or to compromise the faith would have been very great.

There are some characteristics of apocalyptic literature that make it unique. First of all, apocalyptic writing takes the form of visions, and these visions transcend the events of history. While the events of the present for the reader at times seem overwhelming, the visions experienced by the one who records the material go above and beyond the present and take into account all of history and show that God is in control of history. In fact, in Revelation God describes Himself as "the Alpha and the Omega" (Revelation 1:8), using the first and last letters of the Greek alphabet to show that everything from beginning to end is under His control.

It might be said that apocalyptic literature is written in "code." The imagery in the visions and the use of symbolic numbers serve both to uncover (the term *apocalypse,* the Greek title of the Book of Revelation, means "uncovering") and to cover. It uncovers the truth to those who have access to the "code book" needed to decode the writing, while it keeps the truth hidden from the outsider. Such writing is quite useful for giving strength, support, and encouragement to the persecuted, while giving nothing away to the persecutor.

In Revelation, and in apocalyptic literature in general, history is seen as a cosmic battleground in which the forces of good and evil contend for final control of the earth and its inhabitants. There is a very strong dualism here—the forces of evil, Satan and his hosts, are mighty indeed, and at times seem to gain the upper hand. However, victory belongs to God and His hosts, as the forces of evil, which have been overcome by Christ on the cross, are ultimately destroyed.

God has a very good purpose in showing this to us. No matter what struggles we face in our lives, even oppression and persecution, there is a great temptation to compromise our faith, or to lay it aside completely. By showing the ultimate destruction of the forces of evil, God sternly warns us of the consequences of falling away, but at the same time He shows us that if we remain faithful we will receive life with Him. "Be faithful unto death, and I will give you the crown of life" (Revelation 2:10). That very promise gives us the strength to remain faithful, even when times get tough.

It is extremely important to keep the purpose of the book in mind in order not to be distracted by thoughts that the book does not intend to teach. It would be easy to get caught up in the symbolism of the book and try to find a one-to-one correspondence between events in the visions and events going on today, and then decide that this is the only age in which these prophecies could possibly come to pass. Some have gone so far as to create an elaborate scheme of events that "must" come to pass before Christ returns on the basis of a misunderstanding of the purpose of the book. On the other hand, it may be tempting to simply toss the book away as being too bizarre and of no relevance for our time. There is no question but that the book is difficult for our modern sensibilities to lay hold of.

2 Interpreting Revelation

Scholars have offered four different methods of interpreting the Book of Revelation, each based on different assumptions as to the purpose and message of the book.

The first view, known as the "preterist" view, sees the events of the book happening entirely in the past, specifically at the time of John.

The second view, the "futurist" view, sees the entire book, except for the first three chapters, as lying in the future, the events not taking place until immediately before the return of Christ. One form of this is the "dispensational" view, which divides the history of the world into seven "dispensations," or ages, with God dealing with humanity in a different way in each. In this view Revelation is understood to cover the last part of the sixth age and the seventh age.

A third view is the "idealist" view, which sees the book speaking symbolically of such timeless truths as the victory of good over evil.

The fourth view, and the view to be preferred (and which is used in this LifeLight study), is the "historical" view, which sees Revelation presenting in a symbolic manner the entire history of the church from the time of Christ up to the last judgment, and into eternity. In this understanding, the seven visions in Revelation each cover the same period of time—the entire age of the church—each vision describing the same events from a different perspective and adding a little more to what was presented in the earlier visions.

This last understanding is to be preferred because it uses proper methods of interpreting the Scriptures, by using the clear passages of the rest of the Scriptures to interpret a book that by its very nature is unclear, rather than reducing the book to either a historical curiosity or a moralistic treatise, as the preterist and idealist views do, or by using Revelation to interpret the rest of Scripture, as the futurist method does.

3 Historical Background

John, the author of this book, was writing to congregations in danger of persecution, while he himself was already suffering persecution. The John who wrote this book was undoubtedly also the John who wrote the Gospel account and the three letters that bear his name. In the Gospel he is referred to as the disciple whom Jesus loved (John 21:20 and elsewhere).

Tradition has it that John is the only one of the Twelve who did not suffer a martyr's death. This, however, did not mean that he did not suffer persecution. In fact, the vision we have recorded in this book (the title is Revelation, in the singular) was given to him while he was in exile on the island of Patmos, a small rocky island off the coast of Asia Minor, where he had been sent for refusing to compromise his faith. The time is about the year AD 95, over 60 years after the death and resurrection of our Lord. By this time John was quite old and, tradition tells us, had been living in the city of Ephesus, in the Roman province of Asia.

Through the work of Paul and later the work of John, the province of Asia (present-day Turkey) had become the most thoroughly Christian province in the Roman Empire. However, in spite of the great growth of Christianity in the empire, it can by no means be said that the empire had itself been completely Christianized. Far from it! Christians were still at the mercy of the ruling powers. While the Book of Acts notes occasions in which the ruling powers dismissed charges against St. Paul because they were unjust, the government saw its purpose as the preservation of peace, and religion was one means by which peace and order could be maintained.

By the time Revelation was written, Caesar worship was the most widespread and most widely practiced religion of the Roman Empire. This religion actually was not one that had been imposed upon the nation by the rulers but began as a popular movement, expressing the gratitude of the people toward Rome, which had become personified in the goddess Roma, who came to symbolize the state. As the years went on, worship began to shift from Roma to the emperor himself. From time to time emperors were given divine honors after their death, as Caesar Augustus allowed with Julius Caesar.

Other emperors sought to stop the practice, the major exception being Emperor Gaius, better known as Caligula, who ruled from AD 37 to 41. He bestowed divine honors upon himself and even went so far as to attempt to set up a statue of himself in the temple in Jerusalem.

Caligula remained the exception until Domitian, who ruled the Roman Empire from AD 81 to 96. Domitian bestowed divine honors upon himself and his predecessors and gave himself the title "Lord and God." He went so far as to require that once a year all residents of the empire appear before a magistrate and burn a pinch of incense to the emperor as god. If they met this one requirement, they would be allowed to worship any other god or goddess of their own choosing.

How tempting it must have been to offer that one small sacrifice to Caesar and then to be let alone to worship according to one's own conscience! But it was impossible for Christians to offer even that one small pinch of incense, since Jesus Christ was and is their only Lord and God.

The members of the churches in Asia to whom Christ was speaking through John were thus faced with the competing claims of Christ and of one who had set himself up as lord and god. Since Jesus had pointed out that no one can serve two masters, Christians had no option but to refuse to offer this sacrifice. The opening letters to the congregations in Asia, and indeed the whole of the Book of Revelation, come out of the call to remain faithful even in the face of death.

4 Certainty for an Uncertain Future (Revelation 1:1–3)

As we get into the opening verses of Revelation, we can immediately begin to see how the book is to be understood. The opening sentence notes that God gave this revelation to John in order to show "what must soon take place." God desires to give certainty in the midst of an uncertain future, but only on His terms. He will not answer all of our questions, but He will show us that in the midst of seeming defeat we can have hope because the victory has already been won.

That is why those who read this book are called "blessed" (1:3). This term will be used to describe God's people six more times in this book, making a total of seven "beatitudes." God's people will be blessed when they take this book to heart, because "the time is near." The time of persecution, of seeming defeat, has arrived for God's people, and the words of this book provide them with the strength to endure by pointing them to the final victory.

The revelation given to John that comprises the content of this book is given through God's "angel." The angels, ministering spirits who serve God and His people, are mentioned throughout the Scriptures, from Genesis to Revelation, and are active from their singing at the creation of the world (Job 38:7) through their return with Christ at the Day of Judgment (Matthew 25:31). The very word *angel* means "messenger," and one of their most important functions in the Scriptures is that of delivering messages from God that mark momentous events in the deliverance of His people. Examples include the appearance of the "Angel of the Lord" (possibly the pre-incarnate Christ Himself) to the patriarchs and to Moses at the burning bush to call him to lead Israel out of captivity to the Promised Land, to the use of angels in the call of other prophets (for example, Isaiah in Isaiah 6), and the announcement of the coming births of children who would be instrumental in the deliverance both of Old Testament Israel and of the whole world—of Isaac to Abraham and Sarah, of John the Baptist to Zechariah, of Jesus to Mary and to Joseph, culminating in the announcement of the birth of Jesus to the shepherds. Whenever angels speak, the message is to be heard as though coming from the mouth of God Himself.

Angels are active in carrying out God's judgment against the world throughout Revelation, and also are active in the war against the armies of Satan. We see the war between God and Satan waged on two stages—the spiritual stage and the earthly stage. The spiritual battle rages on, and the defeat of Satan marks the real victory. However, members of the human race are not merely pawns in the struggle, but are deeply involved, for the forces of Satan use other human beings in their quest for the destruction of the people of God.

Far from being insignificant, what goes on in the world has great spiritual significance; the eternal salvation of the people of God is at stake. The Revelation to John reminds God's people that God's victory is more than a foregone conclusion—it has already been won through the blood of the Lamb, the Lamb who by His death conquered death. Though Satan is powerful, his defeat is assured.

This revelation comes to John in the midst of this spiritual battle, as the forces of Satan, using the government of the Roman Empire, sought to destroy the church of God, through forcing either apostasy or death. Through apocalyptic imagery, Christians are promised that they already have the victory, even though that victory is visible only through the eyes of faith. This message of hope is conveyed in a way that only Christians can understand, since only Christians have the knowledge that unlocks the code of apocalyptic messages.

5 The Old Testament Key (Revelation 1:4–8)

Already in these opening verses, it becomes clear that the "code book" that unlocks the Revelation to John is nothing other than the Old Testament. Of the 404 verses of Revelation, 278 of them make reference to the Old Testament. To a people familiar with the Old Testament, Revelation was an open book, not a closed one. Rather than showing a division between Old and New Testaments, Revelation shows that they stand together as a continuous stream, the New Testament fulfilling the Old and pointing to the final fulfillment in the return of Christ for judgment.

It is through the Old Testament that the symbolism of the Book of Revelation may be understood. Verse 7, for example, declares that Jesus is "coming with the clouds." This verse refers directly to Daniel 7:13, in which the one like a Son of Man comes in the clouds and approaches the Ancient of Days. Jesus Himself applied this prophecy to Himself, as recorded in Matthew 24:30 and 26:64 and their parallels in Mark and Luke. The declaration later on in the verse that even those who pierced Him will look upon Him is a direct citation of Zechariah 12:10, and alludes also to Isaiah 53:5 and Psalm 22:16.

As we enter into a study of Revelation, we will see many strange creatures and awesome events, but many of them are referred to in the Old Testament as well. When the reader who is familiar with the Old Testament sees the events described here, he or she remembers that God is consistent and that the whole of history is in His hands.

When you recognize the "coded" nature of the Book of Revelation, you can begin to make sense of the various numbers that occur in it. The failure to properly understand the use of numbers in Revelation is responsible for some of the many misuses of the book that have arisen within the church, many of which lead to fear rather than comfort.

The numbers in Revelation are important for understanding the message of the book. The meanings of the numbers remain consistent throughout, and knowing the proper meaning will enable you to see the message. While there is not total agreement among scholars as to the precise meaning of some of the numbers, the following guidelines will help you in seeing the message behind the numbers.

The first significant and common number to appear in Revelation is the number 7, first appearing in verse 4, referring to the seven churches in Asia and the seven spirits before the throne of God. Seven is the number of completeness, perfection, or holiness. The creation of the world culminated with God's resting on the seventh day. The Old Testament speaks of seven high festivals in the Jewish year, four of them falling in the seventh month, and two of them lasting for seven days. The seven churches that are mentioned are real congregations, but they stand for the whole of Christendom, and the seven spirits symbolize the fullness of the power of the Holy Spirit, perhaps referring to the sevenfold description in Isaiah 11:2—He is the Spirit of the Lord, the Spirit of wisdom, of understanding, of counsel, of power, of knowledge, and of the fear of the Lord.

Seven in turn is the sum of two other numbers standing for completeness: 3, which is the number of God (the triune God, Father, Son, and Holy Spirit), and 4, the number of the world (the four directions of the compass). The number 3½, half of 7, is always associated with the evil forces that oppress the church, usually those spiritual and religious in nature. This number comes in several variants as well: "a time, and times, and half a time," in 12:14; 42 months or 1,260 days (three and one-half years) in 11:2–3 and 12:6.

The numbers 12 and 10 are also of great significance. The number 12 refers to Old Testament Israel (the 12 tribes) and New Testament Israel, the church (the 12 apostles). Ten and its cube (10×10×10), 1,000, represent completeness. These may be multiplied and combined to get important illustrative combinations: 24 (Old Testament plus New Testament churches); or 144,000 (12×12×1,000 represents the whole people of God—past, present, and future).

Conclusion

As we move through the book, we will see how these numbers illustrate God's truth to us, how they tell us what must soon take place, and how they are given to us to comfort us in the midst of our struggles in life. This introductory section ends with a resounding note of assurance, as God declares to us that He is the Alpha and the Omega. These are the first and last letters of the Greek alphabet, an appropriate reference, as the book was originally written in Greek. As the first and the last, the one who was, who is, and who is to come, He rules over all human history. These words echo throughout the rest of the book, reminding God's people that He is in control and that the victory has already been won for them. As we move through the book in the coming weeks, may that declaration of hope and of certain victory be uppermost in your minds.

Concluding Activities

As time permits, encourage a number of participants to read their written answers to question 12 regarding the verse they could identify with most closely and to give their reason for doing so. Suggest that someone speak a brief, pertinent prayer.

Then make any necessary announcements and distribute the enrichment magazine. Encourage participants to browse in the magazine and keep it as a helpful reference for coming lessons.

Encourage participants to set a weekly plan for their LifeLight study. A consistent daily schedule works best for most. Some begin or end the day with LifeLight. Others find another time during the day at home or during a break or lunch hour at work. Invite participants to share their practices, especially if your group has some who are new to LifeLight.

The Triumphant Christ Speaks to His Church

Revelation 1:9–3:22

Preparing for the Session

Central Focus

It is a source of joy and comfort to know that Christ gives His message of hope to the church through the ages. Since we live in a sinful world, the church continually struggles with problems from the inside and outside. This week we hear Christ, who has triumphed over all the problems that will ever confront us, even death itself, speaking words of judgment and encouragement to His people and calling them to continued faithfulness.

Objectives

That participants, led by the Holy Spirit, will

1. see that Christ's glorious attributes match the specific needs of each congregation;
2. rejoice in Christ's presence in the midst of His people; and
3. examine their life and the life of their congregation in the light of Christ's standards of judgment as expressed in these letters.

Note for the small-group leaders: Lesson notes and other materials you will need begin on page 58.

For the Director

The most helpful materials the director can provide for the second week are maps of the Middle East, and especially of the Island of Patmos and of the seven cities of Asia Minor scrutinized in the first three chapters of the Book of Revelation. It can make the study much more meaningful if the participants can see the geographical relationships.

For the Lecture Leader

The presentation this week should let the triumphant majesty of Jesus Christ beam forth in His appearance and in His careful analysis of the representative churches mentioned. Help the participants see how fitting Christ's attributes in chapter 1 are to the respective churches in chapters 2 and 3.

Session Plan

Worship

The terms used in this week's Bible study lead us to consider with awe and adoration the triumphant Christ, who guides His church through this world of sin and death.

Psalm 45 is a fitting hymn of praise to the Messiah, and the hymn printed in the leaflet appropriately praises Him who rose from the dead to give us life forever with Him.

If time permits, read Psalm 45. Then continue with the hymn printed in the study leaflet. Accompaniments are available in denominational hymnals, such as *Lutheran Service Book* or *Lutheran Worship* (refer to hymnal index). (Note: Concordia Publishing House has available *The Concordia Organist*. All the initial worship hymns in the LifeLight courses are included in this resource. It's especially helpful for mission congregations and small parishes. See the list of study resources on page 7.)

Prayer

Blessed Savior and Lord, You are the first and the last and the living one. You were dead, and behold You are alive forevermore. We are weak, sinful human beings, but You have revealed Yourself to us as our triumphant living Savior. We trust You and want to live our lives to Your glory. By Your Holy Spirit lead us to do so more and more, for Your name's sake! Amen.

Lecture Presentation

Introduction

John, an apostle of Jesus Christ, was in exile on the island of Patmos in the Aegean Sea because of his testimony for Jesus. Rather than deny his Lord and submit to the emperor's command to honor him as a god, rather than cease preaching the Gospel of the Lord whom he knew and loved, John was willing to go into exile. This certainly was not John's first experience of punishment for testifying of Jesus. Many years previously, back in the city of Jerusalem, John was arrested along with the other apostles for preaching of Christ and was brought before the Sanhedrin, the Jewish high court. When commanded to stop, they refused, and rejoiced because "they were counted worthy to suffer dishonor for the name" (Acts 5:41). John was experiencing what all followers of Jesus may at some time or another be called to experience—suffering persecution for the sake of the Gospel. That he identifies his situation with that of other believers is clear, as he identifies himself as his readers' "brother and partner in the tribulation and the kingdom and the patient endurance" (Revelation 1:9).

It was on the Lord's Day (Sunday) that Christ Himself appeared to John in quite a startling way, inaugurating a series of visions by which Christ would comfort His church. Here the Lord speaks directly to John and begins to tell him what "must soon take place" (Revelation 1:1). This first set of visions is specifically addressed to seven congregations in Asia Minor. The events described, however, have their parallels in every age, and the words are as relevant today as they were at that time, because the human condition and the world's attitude toward the church have not changed in the intervening 1,900 years.

The words that are spoken to each church are words of both warning and encouragement; that is, both Law and Gospel. In every case there is an exhortation to remain faithful and also the promise that Christ will always be with His people, as He promised His disciples before He left them (Matthew 28:20).

1 The Appearance of the Triumphant Christ (Revelation 1:9–20)

The description of the one "like a son of man" who appears to John is striking. Though this being is never referred to as "Jesus" or as "the Christ," there is no doubt about who it is. The description of Jesus given here is quite different from the picture we get in the Gospels. While Jesus is never described physically in the Gospels, apart from His transfiguration in which His divine nature shone forth briefly, here great emphasis is placed on His appearance. But it is clear that this is not a physical description, but rather a spiritual portrayal using physical imagery.

While the description at first seems strange and fantastic, its meaning becomes clear when compared to the Old Testament pictures of God and His Messiah. Thus we see that the God who has revealed Himself in Jesus Christ is the God of all ages. He is the one "like a son of man" who is referred to in Daniel 7:13, the one who comes with the clouds of heaven. He wears a robe down to His feet, the style worn by the high priest of the Israelite religion (Exodus 28:4; 29:5). The golden sash He wears indicates that He occupies the office of high priest, the office ascribed to Jesus throughout the Letter to the Hebrews.

His hair is white like wool, the symbol of wisdom and purity. In Daniel 7 it is the "Ancient of Days" whose hair is "like pure wool," so we see a clear connection between the Son and the Father. What is ascribed in Scripture to the Father is here also ascribed to the Son. What belongs to the "Ancient of Days" likewise belongs to the Son of Man. His eyes are like blazing fire, indicating penetrating insight—nothing escapes His gaze, and all that human beings seek to keep hidden is laid open to the eyes of Christ. His voice has the "roar of many waters," a description given to the voice of God in Ezekiel 43:2. The sash, the eyes, the feet like bronze and the voice all also call to mind the one "having the appearance of a man" who delivers a message to Daniel in Daniel 10.

1:20—As Jesus Himself states, the seven stars in His right hand represent the messengers ("angels") of the churches, most likely the pastors of the churches, and the seven lampstands among which He stands represent the seven churches to whom the seven letters that follow are being sent; by extension these also represent the whole church on earth. Like a lampstand, the church does not produce the light of the world, but it rather bears the Light of the world, Christ Himself. It bears the Light to the world by speaking the Word of God, which has been committed to it. When the Word of God is spoken by His people, it is as though Christ Himself is speaking.

Since the Old Testament (Isaiah 49:2) tells us that the mouth of the servant of God will be made "like a sharp sword," and since the New Testament says that the Word of God is the "sword of the Spirit" (Ephesians 6:17), or is "sharper than any two-edged sword" (Hebrews 4:12), the image of the sword coming out of Christ's mouth is quite appropriate. Our Lord governs the world by no other way than by His Word. The Word of God alone changes the lives of people: it drives us to repentance when it convicts us of our sin through the preaching of the Law, and it gives us hope and comfort and empowers us for service through the Good News that God has been merciful to us by sending Christ to die for us.

The Christ who appears to John by His very appearance shows Himself to be victorious. His face shines like the sun, as it did at His transfiguration, an event that John himself witnessed. When John, quite understandably, falls at the feet of Christ, he hears the words "Fear not." Whenever God acts, whenever people see God as He really is, they naturally become even more aware of their insignificance when compared to the majesty of God, and their wretchedness when compared to the holiness of God, so that they tremble in fear. But for the people of God those words of assurance, "Fear not," come as a great comfort, assuring them that God has put away their sins, that they stand cleansed before God, and that God has declared them to be His people.

The words of Jesus set the stage for the rest of Revelation, because they point to the victory which has already been won. Verse 17—He describes Himself as the First and the Last, echoing the words of 1:8, which are ascribed to the Lord God, thus showing that He and the Father truly are one, as Jesus had declared in John 10:30. Verse 18—His declaration that He was dead and is now alive forever shows that He is *already* victorious. The events to come (which Revelation will reveal in the following visions) show Satan's last-ditch attempts to destroy the work of Christ, to turn the world away from Him. But in the resurrection of Christ it is made clear to us that the victory has already been won—that we need not fear those who can destroy the body but cannot destroy the soul (that is, who can kill us physically but cannot touch us spiritually), because eternal life has already been won for us. The strength to endure whatever the world sends against us comes from knowing the one who has already won the victory. He is the one who has the keys to death and Hades, who has released His people from their power, and who will ultimately condemn the wicked to eternal destruction.

2 The Letters to the Churches (Revelation 2–3)

It is this victorious Lord who speaks to the seven churches of Asia Minor. These churches were real congregations in existence at that time. If you look at a map of Asia Minor, you can see the cities mentioned, and notice that, if you move from city to city, you move in a horseshoe pattern that touches each of the cities in turn, from Ephesus at the southwestern tip to Laodicea at the southeastern tip. These cities all lay on a major thoroughfare, making it possible for the letters to them to be widely disseminated. As major centers of Asia Minor, the worship of the emperor would be especially strong in those cities and the threat of persecution especially strong.

There is no doubt that the problems mentioned were literal problems being experienced by those congregations. Nevertheless, since the number 7 itself indicates completeness, the seven churches themselves, though real congregations, are representative of the entire Christian church of all times and places. The churches of God today all have their challenges, and Satan is as active today in his struggle to destroy the church as he was then. Therefore, the letters to these first-century congregations have relevance for the congregations of today, first in their words of warning and exhortation, but also in their words of comfort and encouragement.

The letters to the seven churches are written in the same format, and a sevenfold division can generally be seen, though in special cases one or more parts may be missing: (1) the greeting; (2) a title of the risen Christ based on the description in chapter 1; (3) a word of praise, beginning "I know"; (4) a criticism; (5) a warning; (6) an exhortation, beginning "He who has an ear"; and (7) a promise, which will reach fulfillment in the closing chapters of the book (Revelation 20–22). Some of the churches are doing well, some have problems brewing, and yet others are in grave spiritual danger.

So it is among the churches of God today. These letters all use God's formula for dealing with His people—praising us for our service, calling us to repentance when we fail to be vigilant, warning us of the outcome should we fall away, and exhorting us to remain faithful. All of this is done in the context of His Lordship over His church and always laying before us the hope that He has won for us—the hope that gives us the strength to endure. Each letter ends with a declaration of the blessing that will belong to the one who "conquers." We know that God's people are "more than conquerors" (Romans 8:37). Faith brings victory because it clings to the one who has already emerged victorious. Those who remain faithful will emerge victorious with their victorious Lord.

A. Ephesus (2:1–7)

The first letter (Revelation 2:1–7) is written to the church at Ephesus. Ephesus was the greatest city in Asia Minor at that time, and it was the center for worship of the goddess Artemis (Diana). The temple to Diana was one of the seven wonders of the ancient world. The church was begun through the preaching of Paul (Acts 19), and the riot that ensued as a result of Paul's preaching of the Gospel shows how the world reacts violently against Christ when it believes that its own interests are being threatened. Nevertheless, Paul had a successful ministry there, and the congregation was well established through his preaching of the Gospel.

Verses 2–3—Christ here praises the congregation for its hard work and its perseverance in the faith—how it refused to tolerate the wicked and tested those who claimed to be apostles, but were not (that is, who were false teachers under the guise of God's servants). In other words, they knew the Word of God and were able to determine who taught according to it and who did not. Like the Bereans to whom Paul preached (Acts 17:11), the Ephesians searched the Scriptures to see if what these men said was so.

Verse 6—They are also praised for hating the practices of the Nicolaitans, a sect that sought to compromise with pagan society, proclaiming that Christian liberty allowed them to practice idolatry and immorality, thus allowing them to avoid suffering for the faith. Such practices must certainly be condemned, for Christ calls us to deny ourselves and our own desires, take up our cross and follow Him (Mark 8:34). The Ephesians were aware of the seriousness of committing their entire beings to Christ, for it might well put them in the way of suffering.

However, while they were commended for their zeal, they were also called upon to repent of forsaking their first love (Revelation 2:4). Their love for Christ and for one another had cooled, and had to be restored, since love is the first fruit of the Spirit (Galatians 5:22). While He was engaged in His earthly ministry, Christ warned the Pharisees of their unloving, self-righteous attitude, pointing out that the heart must be right for the actions to be approved by God. The Ephesians were doing what was outwardly correct, but their hearts were not right, and they were again in danger of falling under God's judgment. Christ called them to continual self-examination and repentance lest they be lost.

The message is one that we need continually to hear today, lest our love also cool and we begin to take Christ's blessings for granted. Remember who and what we are, and what Christ has done for each of us! Then our zeal for the Lord will increase, as will our love for Him and for all for whom He died. Do so, and we, too, will eat of the tree of life, taken away with the fall (Genesis 3:22–24), but to be restored in the new heaven and new earth (Revelation 22:2, 14).

B. Smyrna (2:8–11)

To the church at Smyrna, a powerful and beautiful city in which Greek and Roman culture flourished, Christ has nothing but praise and encouragement. Already being persecuted by some of the Jewish population of the city, they are warned to be prepared for a brief period ("ten days," a short, limited period [v. 10]) of further persecution. Nevertheless, they are told not to be afraid, because by being faithful they will inherit a crown of life. Though they may even have to experience physical death, they are assured that the second death, eternal death, will not touch them.

Though for the most part we today do not experience physical persecution, we nevertheless live in a culture that looks down on and ridicules Christ, His people, and their lifestyle. Therefore, the encouragement not to give in to the surrounding culture is an important message to us. We may be assured that Christ will continue to give us the strength to remain faithful and that such faithfulness will be rewarded with the gift of eternal life.

C. Pergamum (2:12–17)

The city of Pergamum, the northernmost of the seven cities, was the administrative center of the province, and so emperor worship was strictly enforced there. Verse 13—It thus was the city "where Satan's throne is." Jesus was pleased that the church was remaining faithful even though Christians were being put to death there. Verses 14–15—However, they are also warned against tolerating those who "hold to the teaching of Balaam" and of the idolatrous and immoral Nicolaitans. When Balaam was unable to curse Old Testament Israel, he counseled Balak to entice Israel into immorality, thus bringing a curse upon themselves. Thus both groups would tempt the church to compromise with the surrounding culture and would thus bring about the downfall of many in the church.

The world is uncomfortable with those who by their lives show that the behavior of the rest of the world is shameful. Christ warns us about tolerating shameful people, and He calls to repentance those who do such things and those who tolerate them. It is tempting to "flirt" with sin, or to think that, since forgiveness is always available, resisting is not all that important. Verse 17—Not so! As God is holy, so He calls His people also to be holy. To those who continue the fight, Christ promises His heavenly food, that is, eternal life. They will also receive "a white stone, with a new name," which serves as their admission ticket to the heavenly banquet. The "new name" signifies the beginning of new life for those who turn from their old way of life to Christ. Embracing Christ means new life, life that ceases to be enamored with sin and instead despises and repudiates it. (Romans 6:2) "How can we who died to sin still live in it?"

D. Thyatira (2:18–29)

The city of Thyatira was the smallest of the seven cities. It is mentioned in Acts (16:14) as the home of Lydia, Paul's first convert in Philippi. Verse 19—The Christians at Thyatira are praised for growing in love, faith, service, and perseverance, unlike those at Ephesus, who had lost their first love. Verse 20—Nevertheless, they were guilty of tolerating "Jezebel." The name is a code name from the Old Testament given to a false prophetess active in the city. Jezebel was the wife of Ahab, King of Israel, who had actively sought to destroy the worship of the true God among the Israelites and replace it with the worship of Baal. Perhaps the attitude of love being conveyed by the people became misguided and led to tolerance of an evil that should have been cast out from among God's people.

As citizens of a pluralistic society that continually demands tolerance of views and practices that Christians should find intolerable, we find that these words speak to us today as well. The exalted Christ warns these Christians that they were being enticed into both idolatry and adultery. Here the Old Testament theme of idolatry being a spiritual form of adultery, as seen in the writings of Jeremiah, Ezekiel, and Hosea, is proclaimed. Unfaithfulness, both sexual and spiritual, shows contempt rather than love for the one offended and destroys relationships rather than healing them. Verse 22—"Jezebel's" coming destruction is announced, and those who tolerated her behavior are called upon to repent. Genuine love will not tolerate evil, but will condemn it. Those who participate in it must be warned, lest they set themselves up for destruction.

E. Sardis (3:1–6)

The problem in Sardis was spiritual lethargy. Christ declared that, though they had a reputation for being alive, they were in fact dead. He urged them to wake up. It may be that since there were no major problems in the church at Sardis there was nothing to challenge them—nothing to keep them sharp—and as a result they had sunk into a stupor. They looked fine outwardly, but in fact were only going through the motions of the faith.

We Christians dare never think that we "have it made" at any time, because Satan is always ready to catch us unawares. Verses 2–3—Jesus warned those in Sardis that if they did not wake up, the Day of Judgment would come upon them "like a thief," as He had warned His disciples while still on earth (Matthew 24:42–44). Verse 4—He does note that there were still some in Sardis who were "worthy," that is, who still had faith and so were truly active in service for their Lord. Verse 5—To those, Christ gives the promise that they will be "clothed thus in white garments"; dressed in His righteousness.

We who remain in the faith are promised the same and are told that our names will not be blotted from the Book of Life—that is, we will not lose our citizenship in the Kingdom of God. The one who holds the "seven spirits" and the "seven stars" will not let His people fall from His hand. Here Christ repeats the promise He made while on earth, that those who acknowledge Him would be acknowledged by Him before His Father in heaven (Matthew 10:32).

F. Philadelphia (3:7–13)

As with the church at Smyrna, Jesus had nothing but praise for the church in Philadelphia. Though the people of the church were perceived as weak, that is, as having little strength, they had nevertheless remained faithful. The Christians of Philadelphia were being attacked by the "synagogue of Satan," those Jews who refused to acknowledge Jesus as Messiah. But the Christians of Philadelphia were assured that at the Judgment these Jews will be forced to acknowledge that Christ had loved the Christians of Philadelphia. They were encouraged to remain faithful in the future as they had been in the past and were promised that they would be preserved from the hour of trial; that is, they would be kept safe when God pours His wrath upon the world. They, like the church at Pergamum, were promised that they would be inscribed with the new name given from Christ Himself. Their strength in their weakness was the grace of God, given them in His Word. God's strength is indeed made perfect in weakness (2 Corinthians 12:9).

G. Laodicea (3:14–22)

The church at Laodicea was the church in the worst condition of all. They were "lukewarm"; they had no zeal for the Lord at all. Even hostility toward Christ is better than this! At least those who are hostile are showing some passion about their beliefs; passion of any kind was lacking among the Christians of Laodicea. Rather than being concerned about their spiritual welfare and that of others, they instead gloried in their earthly wealth. Though outwardly rich, they were spiritually wretched. Yet, though Christ warned them that if they did not change He would spit them out of His mouth (3:16), He had not yet abandoned them. Christ instead called upon them—indeed pleaded with them—to repent so that they would be restored and would sit with Him on His throne, live and rule with Him.

Verse 20—Such is Christ's incredible love, that He continually seeks out those in danger of losing their lives, to restore them to Himself. What a beautiful, heart-moving plea Christ makes as He stands at the door and knocks, asking for an invitation to come into our hearts!

Conclusion

Though all seven of these cities were prominent at that time, they are no longer significant. Ephesus lies in ruins, and the others for the most part are sparsely populated. The world changes. Cities and nations rise and fall. Through all of these changes, only the Word of God remains. But that Word brings victory to us today as it did to those Christians in their day.

God's people still need to take those warnings to heart, for the temptations of that time remain temptations today. But the promise of victory that has already been won by Christ still is ours today as well.

Concluding Activities

Speak a prayer asking the Holy Spirit to help us "hear what the Spirit says to the churches" (2:11). After the prayer make any necessary announcements. Encourage participants to refer to the enrichment magazine as part of their study.

Our Victorious Lord Leads through Trouble to Triumph

Revelation 4–7

Preparing for the Session

Central Focus

In the serene picture of God's majesty in heaven we see the victorious Lamb taking the scroll and opening the seals to review the future. Here God shows us the destiny of all people: destruction for the wicked and eternal bliss and joy for those who have "washed their robes . . . in the blood of the Lamb."

Objectives

That participants, led by the Holy Spirit, will

1. learn that all history is in God's hands;
2. get a taste of the eternal peace of heaven; and
3. be urged to set their eyes "on things that are above" (Colossians 3:1).

Note for the small-group leaders: Lesson notes and other materials you will need begin on page 61.

For the Director

So much depends on the leadership the director provides, especially in the area of faithful attendance of the participants. If any participant has been absent in the first three sessions, the director should establish personal contact to determine the reason.

For the Lecture Leader

Session Plan

Worship

Begin the session with the hymn printed in the study leaflet. Accompaniments are available in denominational hymnals, such as *Lutheran Service Book* or *Lutheran Worship* (refer to hymnal index). (Note: Concordia Publishing House has available *The Concordia Organist.* All the initial worship hymns in the LifeLight courses are included in this resource. It's especially helpful for mission congregations and small parishes. See the list of study resources on page 7.)

Pray together the prayer in the study leaflet.

Lecture Presentation

Introduction

It is only natural to tremble in the face of an uncertain future. That is why people will do everything they can to divine the future. Astrologers and fortune-tellers thrive because people believe that to know the future is to control it.

The vision of the seven seals shows us that knowledge of the future is sealed from our sight. Yet, through this vision, we see that God Himself is in control of all of history and that Christ Himself has earned the right to open the seals and to reveal the future to us. He does not tell us everything we would like to know. However, He *does* tell us all we need to know to be assured that Christ has already triumphed over the evil powers at work in the world, and that His people will be preserved from all spiritual harm even in the midst of the worst catastrophes that will come upon the world.

1 A Glimpse of Heaven (Revelation 4:1–11)

The vision begins as John is invited to look through an open door into the throne room of heaven. Very few human beings have had that privilege while still living on earth. Several of the Old Testament prophets did. Isaiah, Ezekiel, and Daniel all describe the majesty of heaven and describe its inhabitants (Isaiah 6; Ezekiel 1; Daniel 7). In the New Testament only Paul hints at having had the experience, and he refuses to describe what he saw (2 Corinthians 12). Now John is granted that experience. Verse 2—John again describes himself as being "in the Spirit," that is, in a state of spiritual ecstasy, but with full consciousness.

The center of this vision is the "one seated on the throne" (4:2)—none other than God Himself. Since no one can see God and live (Exodus 33:20), and since

He dwells in "unapproachable light, whom no one has ever seen or can see" (1 Timothy 6:16), the one on the throne is described only in terms of the glow of precious stones—the green of jasper and the red of carnelian, mentioned in the Old Testament as the first and last of the 12 stones on the breastplate of the priests—and His throne is surrounded by a rainbow (mentioned also in Ezekiel 1:26–28), said to be like emerald. As God placed His rainbow in the sky as a sign of His covenant with Noah, so also it here serves as a sign of His covenant with His people.

The seven lamps are the seven spirits, that is, the Holy Spirit, who is coequal in majesty with the Father and the Son. While God Himself is not seen, His presence on His throne echoes the many Old Testament passages, particularly from Psalms, that refer to God enthroned in the heavens, that is, in total charge of His creation and alone worthy of honor. From the throne come flashes of lightning and peals of thunder, signs of the presence and majesty of God. These occur throughout Revelation as heralds of events taking place in the heavenly temple. From His appearance at Mount Sinai (Exodus 19:16) onward, God often made Himself known in the midst of thunder and lightning, reminding the people that He is a God to be held in awe.

Verse 4—Surrounding the throne are the 24 elders, wearing white robes and gold crowns, signifying the 12 patriarchs and the 12 apostles, the heads of the people of God in the Old and New Testaments. They thus represent the church in its totality. They also are seated on thrones and they wear crowns, showing that they live and reign with God Himself, as Christ promised would be the case with His people (cf. 20:4). They are dressed in white, having been clothed in the righteousness of the Lamb, who will soon make His appearance.

Verse 6—Before the throne is the sea of glass, showing God's holiness and His Lordship over all things. He rules over His creation; He is not part of it. Also present are the mysterious "four living creatures," who represent all creation—the wild and domesticated animals of the land, the birds of the air, and humanity. The six wings call to mind the seraphim, angelic beings Isaiah saw in his vision of God's throne room (Isaiah 6:2), and the faces are those of the "living creatures" of Ezekiel 1, who in Ezekiel 10 are called "cherubim." They are covered with eyes, indicating that they see everything; nothing escapes their attention.

The task of these angelic beings is to serve God, first of all through their singing and adoration, which they do continually. They sing the song the seraphim sing in Isaiah 6, which has become the song of the church through the ages: "Holy, holy, holy is the Lord God Almighty" (Old Testament: "the LORD of hosts," i.e., Lord of Armies), "who was and is and is to come!" God declares His name to be "I AM WHO I AM" (Exodus 3:14–15), and His rule is not only now, but extends "from everlasting to everlasting" (Psalm 90:2).

As three is the number of God, so this thrice threefold hymn of praise proclaims the glory of the triune God. To this song the elders, and so all of God's people, respond by laying their crowns before God, declaring that all they have and are comes from God Himself. They testify that God alone is worthy of all glory—no creature, not even the emperor himself, is worthy of such glory, honor, and power, for only God is the creator of all things.

This glimpse into heaven provides the backdrop for the rest of the book. The God who created the heavens and earth rules over His creation. He alone is worthy of honor, and, in the end, He alone will receive it.

2 The Scroll and the Lamb (Revelation 5:1–14)

From the glorious panorama of the throne room of God, John's attention is now called to the scroll that God holds in His right hand. The scroll tells what "must soon take place" (1:1; 4:1); that is, it holds the future. That word *must* has great significance in the New Testament, carrying with it the sense of inevitability, not in the sense of blind fatalism, but in recognizing that because God has decided, it must be so. As Christ carried out His work on earth, He declared, "The Son of Man *must* suffer many things and be rejected" (Mark 8:31).

Verse 2—No human being, indeed no creature, has the right to open the seal and see what is to come; nor can any mere creature bring it about. The cry of the angel, "Who is worthy to open the scroll and break its seals?" is met with silence, leading John to weep because no one was found worthy to open the seals, reveal the future, and set in motion God's plan of salvation for the world.

Verse 5—No one is worthy—except One! As the elder announces, "the Lion of the tribe of Judah" (see Genesis 49:9–10), "the root of David" (see Isaiah 11:1), who is the Lamb of God, is worthy to open the seals. He is worthy because He has triumphed over Satan and death. While no creature may be worthy, by His triumph the Lamb has won a victory that enables Him to show the future to the people of God—a future that will bring about in time the victory already won for eternity.

The image of Jesus as lamb, though rare elsewhere in the New Testament, is permeated with Old Testament imagery. The lamb was a sacrificial animal whose blood was shed for atonement. Most significant was the Passover lamb, whose shed blood marked the doorposts of God's people in Egypt, thus preserving them from death. These sacrificial lambs foreshadowed the death of Jesus, the Lamb of God, the shedding of whose blood was a sacrifice that needed to be made only once for the sins of the whole world. Thus Paul could call Christ our Passover lamb (1 Corinthians 5:7). God in His wisdom, and to further show His control of history, let His Son be put to death on the day of Passover.

The Passover lamb fulfilled its purpose by shedding its blood and dying. So did the Lamb of God. But the Lamb who was slain now stands before the throne of God, risen and victorious. Here we see the Lamb's spiritual attributes set forth in physical language. He stands in the center of the throne, that is, at the seat of God Himself, and not in the position of a creature. Having "humbled Himself," becoming "obedient to the point of death, even death on a cross" (Philippians 2:8), He now has been given back all the honor He forsook for our sake.

Verse 6—He is described in terms of seven, the number of completeness—seven horns (all-powerful) and seven eyes (all-seeing), which are the seven spirits.

Jesus had declared that He had to return to the Father in order that the Holy Spirit might come (John 16:7). In the lamps before the throne and in the eyes of the Lamb we see that the Holy Spirit proceeds from the Father and from the Son. Since Christ's ascension the sevenfold Spirit has been sent out into all the world to proclaim the victory the Lamb has won.

Verse 7—Thus the victorious Lamb, the one who had been slain, takes the scroll from the right hand of God and prepares to open the seven seals. Verse 8—Then the honor and glory, which in chapter 4 were given to the one on the throne, are given in turn to the Lamb. Verses 9–10—All of the beings around the throne join in the song and are accompanied by the prayers of the saints. First comes the song of praise to the Lamb because of the work He has performed on our behalf. By His death He purchased people "from every tribe and language and people and nation"—four groups, four being the number of the world—and made them "a kingdom and priests" (1 Peter 2:5, 9, echoing Exodus 19:6 and Zechariah 3).

Verses 11–12—This new song is then followed by a song sung by the innumerable angel hosts, who give to the Lamb all that rightfully belongs to Him, reaching a climax in 5:12 with the seven attributes of honor, thus saying all that can be said. Verses 13–14—Then all of creation joins in, giving honor to the one on the throne and the Lamb together, once again showing that they live and reign in majesty coequal. The best response to all of this splendor that we can give, other than to say "Amen," is to join in the eternal praise of God with the "angels and archangels, and with all the company of heaven" (*Lutheran Worship*, pp. 146–48).

3 The Opening of the Seals (Revelation 6:1–17)

Verse 1—Though the victorious Lamb is the one who opens the seals, it is not triumph, but rather calamity, that is first revealed. The opening of the first four seals releases in sequence the infamous "four horsemen of the apocalypse," whose coming is announced each in turn by the four living creatures. These horsemen would have been recognized by those familiar with the Old Testament, as similar imagery appears in Zechariah 1:8–17 and 6:1–8. They are powers of the earth whom God uses as His agents of judgment upon the earth. The colors of the horses each signify the character of the rider, and each points to one form of judgment that will strike the earth in the days before God brings this world to an end.

Verse 2—The first horseman is a conqueror, riding a white horse, the symbol of purity and of victory. While his description is similar to that of Christ in 19:15, he is but an imitation, allowed for a time to set himself up as a ruler of this world—hence, an antichrist, that most blatant symbol of human pride, who seeks to be honored as God. His weapon is the bow, the weapon of Gog, the enemy of the people of God mentioned in Ezekiel 38–39. That he comes into the world should be no surprise, since Christ Himself warned of the coming of false Christs (Matthew 24:4–5).

Verse 4—The second horseman, riding a red horse, brings bloodshed to the world with his sword, as he takes peace from the world and causes people to turn against one another in warfare. Again, this should be no surprise, as Christ declared that in the last days there would be "wars and rumors of wars" (Matthew 24:6). Verse 5—The third horseman, riding a black horse, is famine, which follows in the wake of warfare. He carries a pair of scales, indicating the care with which the precious remaining food is doled out among the people. The voice from among the four living creatures shows the great value of the basic needs of life when they become hard to attain. Verses 7–8—The fourth horseman, riding a pale horse, is Death, followed by Hades. How can such calamities as conquest, bloodshed, and famine end, except in death?

Verse 8—The four horsemen are given power over "a fourth of the earth," that is, they do not reign over the whole world, but only a portion, albeit a significant portion. Human beings might be persuaded (falsely) to think that death by old age might somehow be "natural," but death by calamity, sword, famine, and plague show death as the enemy that it really is. These horrors occur in the world as a result of the curse that has come upon creation because of human sin. Not only has sin brought death itself into the world, but sinful people become God's agents in carrying out His judgment upon the world within its history, in preparation for the final judgment.

Verse 9—With the opening of the fifth seal, the scene moves from earth to heaven. Here we see the souls "under the altar," that is, those whose lives have been poured out like sacrificial blood because of their faith. Verse 10—Seeing the turmoil on earth that continues without letup because of human wickedness, including the persecution of the people of God, these souls cry out "How long?" How much longer must this wickedness be tolerated? How much longer before God finally intervenes and vindicates His people?

Verse 11—God replies by telling them to be patient. These saints have already received the white robe, which is the righteousness of Christ, and there is more to come. God does not believe that "justice delayed is justice denied." God delays His justice so that His mercy can be displayed on even more people. Though the wait seems long, God will not bring things to an end until the number of those who would be put to death as they had been is completed. But, He assures them, they will be vindicated. Those who falsely accused the people of God of folly, and put them to death for it, will be shown the folly of *their* ways and will themselves be destroyed. In the midst of the horrors of this world, God remains in control.

Verse 12—Then, with the opening of the sixth seal, God begins His final judgment. The very foundations of the universe will be shaken—the earth with the earthquake, and the sky as sun and moon are darkened and the stars fall from the sky. Then the sky recedes "like a scroll" (Isaiah 34:4), as God rips the heavens open and comes down (cf. Isaiah 64:1). Verse 15—Then the people of this world—there are seven classes listed, signifying completeness—turn and run as they seek to hide themselves from God. The wrath of God is so terrible that even being covered by the mountains would be preferable to facing it.

So many people today seek to minimize the wrath of God and reject the idea that God will pour out His wrath upon impenitent evildoers. But God takes evil seriously. God has declared that He does not desire the death of the wicked but would rather have them turn from their sins and live. He does indeed love the sinner—so much, in fact, that He gave His Son for them. Nevertheless, for those who persist in their rebellion against God, it is certain that the wrath of God rests upon them. When that day of wrath comes, no one can stand.

4 The People of God on Earth and in Heaven (Revelation 7:1–17)

The picture then shifts from those who stand under the wrath of God to the people of God. The angels of God hold back the four winds (four being the symbol of the world), which is God's destructive power sent out against the world (Jeremiah 49:36). The powers of destruction are not unleashed until the servants of God are sealed by God. These are 144,000 in number: 12×12×10×10×10. The number of the church squared times the cube of 10, signifying completeness. These are not 144,000 specific individuals, but represent the entire Christian church on earth.

Note that these verses do not indicate that the people of God will be removed from the world before the end. Rather, they show that God preserves His people in the midst of His judgment. He knows His own, and He protects them. He has marked them with His seal (2 Corinthians 1:22; Ephesians 1:13), the Holy Spirit, through the Sacrament of Baptism. Thus, while they are not preserved *from* the suffering the world endures because of sin, they are preserved *in the midst* of it, and they are preserved by nothing other than the Word of God. As the terrors of war surround them, the people of God remember that God "breaks the bow and shatters the spear" (Psalm 46:9). Though death and Hades are loose in the world, the people of God remember that Christ holds the keys of death and Hades (Revelation 1:18).

The list of the 12 tribes given here does not match any other list in Scripture. The landed tribes would exclude Levi, the tribes of Joseph would be *Ephraim* and Manasseh, and the tribe of Dan would be included in the list of Old Testament tribes. Perhaps Dan is excluded because of its frequent association with idolatry. After all, this list describes spiritual Israel, not Israel according to the flesh. Of the true Israel the Antichrist has no part. Whatever the reason, the knowledge that God preserves all of His people on earth, even through death, is of utmost importance.

After verse 8 the scene shifts again, moving from the church on earth to the church in heaven. Verse 9—Here the people of God are described as "a great multitude that no one could number, from every nation, from all tribes and peoples and languages," the same four groups mentioned in 5:9, though in different order. The multitude stands clothed in the righteousness of Christ and stands before the throne, as did the heavenly chorus in chapter 4. Here, finally, the triumph won through the death of the Lamb is realized in all of its fullness. What God has promised has been brought to pass. The saints have come through the tribulation, the judgment that will come upon the world at the end of its history as described in chapter 6, prophesied by both Daniel (Daniel 12:1) and Jesus (Matthew 24:21). Preserved through their trials, they will live and serve God for eternity.

Their eternal state is described in terms of the miseries of this world, which they will no longer experience. They will no longer know hunger, thirst, or scorching heat, but instead will be led to springs of living water, as Christ had promised (John 4:14). As the children of Israel experienced such troubles as pilgrims in the desert, waiting to enter the Promised Land, so the people of God in every age will experience trials as they wait to enter God's rest. But at long last the pilgrimage will come to an end and sorrow will give way to joy, for God will wipe away every tear from their eyes, those tears they had shed in their suffering in this world.

Conclusion

So the scene ends in heaven, where it all began. These things "must" take place, in order that God's justice may be meted out and His people vindicated. The terrors of this life are real and they are disturbing, but the people of God can look at them and see the hand of God behind them. We can be assured that God can take the evils of the world and use them for His own good purposes. What causes the world to tremble in fear can be for us a reminder of the joy that awaits us. For Christ has told us, "When these things begin to take place, straighten up and raise your heads, because your redemption is drawing near" (Luke 21:28).

Concluding Activities

Close with prayer, perhaps thanking God for preserving us in these difficult times through His Word. Then distribute study leaflet 4 after making any necessary announcements.

The World Shaken, God's Kingdom Stands Firm

Revelation 8–11

Preparing for the Session

Central Focus

We know that God is firmly in control of history. When we look at the world around us, however, it sometimes seems as though this is not the case. In our Bible study this week, we see that even though the world seems to be falling apart around us, God's kingdom stands firm and secure.

Objectives

That participants, led by the Holy Spirit, will

1. continue to be aware of signs of disturbance and destruction being present in every age of world history;
2. be convinced that "the kingdom of the world has become the kingdom of our Lord"; and
3. be grateful for the constant evidence of the triumph of the kingdom of God.

Note for the small-group leaders: Lesson notes and other materials you will need begin on page 64.

For the Lecture Leader

Session Plan

Worship

Begin the session with the hymn printed in the study leaflet. Accompaniments are available in denominational hymnals, such as *Lutheran Service Book* or *Lutheran Worship* (refer to hymnal index). (Note: Concordia Publishing House has available *The Concordia Organist.* All the initial worship hymns in the LifeLight courses are included in this resource. It's especially helpful for mission congregations and small parishes. See the list of study resources on page 7.)

Continue with the prayer printed in the study leaflet.

Lecture Presentation

Introduction

The stability of the world lulls many people into a false sense of security, leading them to think that this rock-solid earth will last forever. Then, disaster strikes somewhere in the world, a reminder that this world will not last forever. The vision of the trumpets in Revelation shows us that such natural disasters occur in accordance with God's plan. In order for people to look at themselves and repent, their security must be destroyed.

When we look in the Gospels at Christ's description of things to come and compare His words to the visions presented to John, it becomes clear that these visions do not describe a series of judgments poured out on the world one after the other; rather, each vision describes the history of the world from Christ's ascension into heaven until the end of the world, each from a different standpoint.

The vision of the seven seals thus shows the world falling apart as sin brings misery to the human race. Now this set of visions, that of the seven trumpets, looks at the same history from the standpoint of the judgment of God. God's hand is seen bringing judgment because of human sin. The very foundations of the earth are shaken, as the forces of nature execute God's judgment. The purpose? To drive the inhabitants of the earth to repentance, to show the fragility of life on earth and the danger of making success in this world the ultimate goal of our lives. Thus, these violent activities also serve as a reminder to God's own children not to put their trust in the world. At the same time, by faith we see beyond the powers shaking the world to the unshakable God who is the Creator of all, and the One who stands firm in the promises He has made to His children.

1 A Golden Censer (Revelation 8:1–5)

Chapter 8 begins by bringing the vision of the seven

seals to an end with the opening of the seventh seal. The opening of this seal inaugurates the next set of visions, that of the seven trumpets. The opening of the seal is greeted with a half-hour silence, by which point all who are caught up in it cannot help but be ready for that which is to come.

Now the preparations take place in heaven for the drama that will be played out on earth. Seven angels are handed seven trumpets, which were used from ancient times as a herald—the sound of the trumpet calls attention to momentous announcements and the onset of momentous events. Seven trumpets were sounded to bring about the fall of the walls of the wicked city of Jericho. Indeed, the end of the world will be heralded with the sound of the "trumpet of God" (1 Thessalonians 4:16), which will truly be the last trumpet (1 Corinthians 15:52). The return of Christ and the resurrection of the dead will be the events that bring this age to a close.

But the time for the last trumpet has not yet come. Instead, the seven angels around the throne who do God's bidding are called upon to announce the seven aspects of the judgment of God that make up God's complete judgment upon the world. But before the sound of the trumpets begins, yet another angel comes, bringing a censer in order to offer incense to God, which ascends to God with the prayers of the saints.

In Revelation 5:8, the servants of God in heaven also bore the prayers of the saints to God in the form of incense. When the saints under the altar cried out "How long?" (6:9–10), they were told to wait. Now, as the prayers of the saints again are brought before God, calling for vindication and for justice, God says, "Now!" as He begins to bring about His judgment upon the world. Verse 5—The angel with the censer fills it with fire from the altar and hurls it to earth, and lightning, thunder, and quaking earth foreshadow God's actions against an evil world. Then, one by one, the trumpets are sounded.

2 The First Four Trumpets (Revelation 8:6–13)

Verse 7—At the sound of the first trumpet a mixture of hail, fire, and blood pour down upon the world. These events call to mind the seventh plague, which was directed against the Egyptians (Exodus 9:13–26). The parallels between the events following the trumpet blasts and the plagues that God visited upon Egypt indicate that through these events God is preparing to free His people from their bondage in this world and lead them to the home He has promised them.

No mention is made yet about the effect on people; only about the effect of this act of judgment on the world. One third of the earth, trees, and grass are burnt up. Here the effect is more severe than that of the fourth seal (6:8), but the effect is still not complete destruction. These events occur to serve as a warning to the world about the strength of God's anger and the coming severity of His judgment, but are not yet God's complete judgment.

Verse 8—At the sound of the second trumpet, a fiery mountain (an image used by Jeremiah to describe the destructive power of Babylon [51:25]) is cast into the sea, a third of which then turns to blood, an act reminiscent of the first plague on Egypt (Exodus 7:20–21). Now a third of the creatures living in the sea are destroyed, and a third of the ships on the seas. No doubt the result would be as Jesus described the last days: "Nations [will be] in perplexity at the roaring of the sea and the waves" (Luke 21:25). Again, the judgment is severe, but it is not final.

Verses 10–11—At the sound of the third trumpet a blazing star falls to earth, which turns a third of the fresh water on earth bitter, that is, makes it undrinkable, leading to the death of many who drink it. In the wilderness, God sweetened the bitter waters at Marah (Exodus 15:25) as a sign for His people. Here, he turns sweet water bitter as a sign against those who reject Him.

Verse 12—At the sound of the fourth trumpet the signs of God's judgment touch the sky. A third of the sun, the moon, and the stars are darkened. God put the lights in the sky as a sign to mark the days and the seasons (Genesis 1:14); now they serve as a sign that God has the power to bring the seasons to an end, further undermining human security in this life. The events here also call to mind the ninth plague on Egypt, the plague of darkness (Exodus 10:21–23).

Thus far, the judgment of God has struck nature and has struck it completely (again, four is the number of the world). The land, the waters of the sea, the waters of the land, and indeed the very heavens themselves, have declared God's judgment. Thus far, people have been affected only as a result of these phenomena in nature. But now things are going to change. The change is marked by the eagle flying through the air, with his cry, "Woe, woe, woe!"

Verse 13—The cry "Woe," used by the Old Testament prophets and by Jesus Himself, is a cry both of judgment and lament. It laments the necessity of judgment and declares that judgment to be inevitable if the people do not repent. Thus it also serves as a cry of warning to the people that they must repent in order to avoid God's righteous judgment. The cry of the eagle thus declares that the three final trumpets will usher in a series of calamities far worse than the ones that have gone before and that these acts of judgment will strike human beings directly.

3 The Final Trumpets (Revelation 9)

As the events of the final trumpets unfold, we see God unleashing the forces of evil upon the world. These forces will plague the world with increasing intensity, but they will do so only at God's command. Though they bring chaos and destruction to the world, it is clear that they do so only because God permits it for His own purposes.

Many scholars from the early church onward have interpreted the blasts of the seven trumpets as the unleashing of false teachings upon the world; these obscure the Gospel and thus destroy human lives. Such an interpretation would certainly be compatible with the events following the final blasts of the trumpet, as supernatural forces of evil are released upon the world.

Verse 1—At the sound of the fifth trumpet, a star, serving as an agent of God, falls to earth, with a key to open the bottomless pit—the abyss—that is, the home of the demons, hell itself. Though their "home," it is clearly also their place of punishment, their confinement, indeed, their prison, as seen in 1 Peter 3:19. When Jesus confronted the legion of demons in the Gerasene demoniac, they begged Jesus not to send them into the abyss (Luke 8:31), that is, not to send them back to hell. Thus, though the abyss is their place of confinement, God in His sovereignty may allow them to work on earth, but their power is limited to what God will allow. Therefore, when the demonic forces are released from the abyss, it is God who allows them to bring their devastation on the earth. Whether they like it or not, they are instruments of God's judgment. God can use even His enemies to bring about His will.

Verse 2—The sound of the fifth trumpet brings the first woe. Smoke arises from the bottomless pit, which darkens the sun (a theme we have seen before and will see again). Out of the smoke comes a plague of locusts. Locusts had been a sign of God's judgment upon Egypt at the time of Moses (Exodus 10:1–20, the eighth plague) and by the prophets Amos (Amos 7:1–3) and Joel (Joel 1:2–2:11) as well. When locusts arrive, they leave nothing but destruction in their wake. It is quite appropriate that their "king" is known as the Destroyer, yet this king of theirs has no real power, for it is God who has released them, and it is God who sets the limits of their power. Joel's imagery of the plague as an army comes to mind here, as these supernatural locusts have human faces and are described as an army ready for battle. These locusts strike only people without God's seal, so that they suffer, but do not die. They are allowed to plague humanity for five months, a period of time suggested by the life cycle of the locust.

What is the nature of this plague? It may well be the plague of a guilty conscience, the deepest and most unbearable pain known to humanity. Far deeper than mere physical pain, it has driven people to long for death, indeed to seek it. Anything is more bearable than to be confronted in our sins by the most holy God! The hosts of evil seek to capitalize on this, increasing the sting of the Law and continually fostering a sense of hopelessness, driving people more and more deeply into despair.

Verse 13—The sound of the sixth trumpet brings the second woe. Now four angels who are in charge of a vast army are released to kill one third of humanity. The snakelike attributes given to this army show its demonic origins. Again, God allows the demonic hordes to do their work, even to bring about death, but for His own purposes. His purposes include not only judgment, but also repentance. God must use drastic measures, even the forces of evil themselves, to confront people with the seriousness of their sin so that they might turn from it. Nevertheless, even in the face of destruction, people will of their own accord remain attached to the very things that have brought destruction upon them. On the Day of Judgment they will not be able to claim ignorance of their sinfulness, for it has clearly been set before them. Nevertheless, such will be their cry: "We never knew!" Such is the nature of human blindness.

4 The Little Scroll (Revelation 10)

The sequence of events leading to the end is interrupted with an interlude marked by the appearance of the angel with the little scroll. Verse 1—This angel is described with images of God's covenant with His people: the rainbow given to Noah, the pillars of cloud and fire that led Israel through the wilderness, the face shining as the sun as did the face of our Lord, the Sun of Righteousness, at His transfiguration. Verses 2–3—This angel, planting one foot on the land and the other on the sea, showing that his message affects the destiny of all of creation, gives a shout like the roar of a lion, perhaps even the Lion of Judah himself. At his shout the seven thunders, the complete judgment of God, speak. Yet the time for that judgment has not yet come, and so their words are sealed up until that time.

Verse 9—Now, however, it is time for John to take the little scroll, and not read it, but eat it. In the church's traditional Collect for the Word, we ask that we might "read, mark, learn, and take [God's Word] to heart" (*Lutheran Worship*, p. 156). To compare that prayer to this account is not merely a cute play on words but shows how the Word, which comes from outside of the prophet, must also become a part of him as he prepares to continue to prophesy to the world. As Jeremiah did poetically (Jeremiah 15:16) and Ezekiel did literally (Ezekiel 2:8–3:3), John takes the scroll and eats it as commanded. As with Ezekiel, this scroll tastes sweet in his mouth, but turns his stomach sour.

The opportunity to speak God's Word is always sweet, though the words may be bitter, as they were in Ezekiel's case, or though the result may be bitter—rejection and persecution rather than acceptance, as was the case with Jeremiah. Such will always be the case with those called upon to bring God's Word to the world, as they continue to prophesy about peoples, nations, tongues, and kings.

5 The Two Witnesses (Revelation 11:1–14)

The world's response to those who prophesy in God's name is shown in the next scene, in the account of the two witnesses, a vision with images derived both from the Old Testament and from John's contemporary world. John is called upon to measure the temple of God and the altar and to count the worshipers. In Ezekiel 40–48 the prophet describes in detail the temple of God, the temple that includes only the people of God, a temple that has never been built on this earth. In 2 Corinthians 6:16 Paul refers to the New Testament church as the temple of God. Here in the inner sanctuary only those who are pure, who have been clothed in the righteousness of Christ, have been admitted. While the events that follow take place, the true church rests under God's protection.

The outer court, however, has been handed over to the Gentiles, in this case those who claim to be people of God but in reality are not. Recall Jesus' words of warning about "those who say that they are Jews and are not, but are a synagogue of Satan" (2:9). Though they claim to be believers they are in fact unrighteous. Indeed, they are not just content to live in their own unrighteousness, but will do everything possible to blot out the call to true repentance.

As in Jeremiah's time, so also until the end of the age is the Word of God attacked even by those who claim to be children of God. The "holy city," holy because of its association with the temple, but now having more in common with Sodom, will be trampled upon for 42 months, that is, three and a half years, that symbol of the time of Satan's attacks against the church, namely the entire age of the church; and the two witnesses will prophesy among the unrighteous for that same period of time, now called 1,260 days, but will not be killed until their testimony is complete, that is, until all have heard the Gospel.

These two witnesses are called "olive trees," as were God's witnesses Zerubbabel, the civil ruler, and Joshua, the high priest, at the time of the return from the Babylonian captivity (Zechariah 4:1–14). As vehicles of the Spirit of God, they are also called "lampstands," as the seven churches of Asia Minor were earlier (1:20). According to Jewish law, two witnesses are necessary to convict a person of a crime (Deuteronomy 19:15). These two witnesses, therefore, are the minimum necessary to convict those who claim to be citizens of the "holy city," but who in fact are enemies of God.

Rather than seeing these two witnesses as specific individuals who will come to the world when the time of the end is near, we should understand the witnesses as being the Word of God itself, which will be proclaimed in the world as long as the world lasts. Nevertheless, the description of these two witnesses calls to mind Moses, who stood alone among the Egyptians, who called down plagues upon the nation until God's people were freed, and Elijah, who dried up the skies to express God's judgment against King Ahab of Israel (1 Kings 17:1) and who called down fire from heaven at Mount Carmel (1 Kings 18:16–45). Though constantly threatened, neither was put to death by the enemies of God.

Yet what evil people do not dare to do, Satan himself has the arrogance to attempt. As the end draws near, these two witnesses will be put to death by the beast from the abyss, Satan himself. He will think that he has finally stopped the preaching of God's Word and that thereby he has snuffed out the last vestige of the kingdom of God on earth and has emerged victorious, able to claim the world for himself. But after three and a half days of revelry, in which the citizens of this supposedly great city show their disgust for the witnesses by allowing their bodies to remain in the street, they are brought back to life by the breath of God. Their work completed, they are taken up into heaven, as Moses was after his death, as Elijah was without dying. They are taken up in a cloud as was the Lord Himself after His resurrection.

Once again the divine hand behind these events is seen in the occurrence of an earthquake. Those who survive the earthquake give glory to God. With the people who witnessed God's defeat of Baal on Mount Carmel through the prophet Elijah, these people must shout, "The LORD, He is God!" (1 Kings 18:39). The cry may come from repentance, or it may come as acknowledgement of the enemy who has conquered them. But one way or another, at the end of the world, "every knee should bow" and "every tongue confess" that the Lord is God (Philippians 2:10–11; Isaiah 45:23).

6 The Seventh Trumpet (Revelation 11:15–19)

Verse 15—With the completion of the second woe, the seventh trumpet is sounded. At the sound of the final trumpet, "The kingdom of the world has become the kingdom of our Lord and of His Christ." Verses 16–18—The song of the elders now simply refers to the Lord God Almighty as the One "who is and who was" (and not "who is to come")—for He has now in fact come. The time of trial for the people of God is past; the time of judgment for the enemies of God has come. The faithful will be vindicated and rewarded, the servants of the Destroyer will be destroyed. The judgment is again revealed from heaven with the revealing of the ark of the covenant, the sign of God's presence with His people from the wanderings in the wilderness to the end of the monarchy. Verse 19—As always, that presence is accompanied by lightning, thunder, rumblings, earthquake, and hail, as God shakes the sinful world to its very foundations.

Conclusion

The world is filled with uncertainty. The destructive forces of nature fill people with dread when they strike, forcing people to come to terms with their own mortality and that of the very universe itself. People turn every way to seek something that will give them certainty. Yet human nature, when confronted with God's Word, will seek to destroy it rather than believe it. Nevertheless, God's Word continues to be proclaimed in the world, driving people to repentance and comforting them with the knowledge that through Christ they are in God's hands. The Word of God stands firm in the midst of the instability of the world, and God keeps His people safe, even as the world rejects them and the message they proclaim.

Concluding Activities

If time permits, close by reading Psalm 2. Then distribute study leaflet 5 after making any necessary announcements.

Christ's Victory over Satan and His Hosts

Revelation 12–14

Preparing for the Session

Central Focus

God is in charge, but Satan persists in trying to defeat Him. This week we see that Satan is vigorously and persistently at work seeking to overthrow God's kingdom and to deceive His people. But we also see that God preserves His people from the strongest assaults of the evil one and his servants and keeps them safe.

Objectives

That participants, led by the Holy Spirit, will

1. see how Satan seeks to overthrow Christ;
2. become more confident of Christ's power to overcome Satan and his hosts; and
3. point others to the victory that Christ has already won over Satan and his hosts.

Note for the small-group leader: Lesson notes and other materials you will need begin on page 67.

For the Lecture Leader

Session Plan

Worship

Begin the session with the hymn printed in the study leaflet. Accompaniments are available in denominational hymnals, such as *Lutheran Service Book* or *Lutheran Worship* (refer to hymnal index). (Note: Concordia Publishing House has available *The Concordia Organist*. All the initial worship hymns in the LifeLight courses are included in this resource. It's especially helpful for mission congregations and small parishes. See the list of study resources on page 7.)

Pray together the prayer printed in the study leaflet.

Lecture Presentation

Introduction

Many people have a great fascination with the occult and the demonic. The use of mediums, Tarot cards, horoscopes, and other means of foretelling the future seems to be increasing. It is clear from the Scriptures that association with such things is forbidden by God, since the future clearly lies in the hands of God, and we are to put our trust in Him rather than to try to divine the future and thereby gain control of it for our own ends.

Even more ominous is the increased preoccupation with Satan himself, which has grown rapidly ever since the book and movie versions of *The Exorcist* in the early 1970s. There is evidence of a rise in Satanic worship quite often among those people who feel utterly powerless as they face the world around them and who see Satan as a power they can tap into to give them power.

Satan, the old liar that he is, certainly encourages people to think that way. In *Paradise Lost* the poet Milton has Satan declare, "Better to reign in hell than serve in heaven." But Satan most certainly does not "reign" in hell; he is very much a prisoner there himself. Those he deceives will not rule with him, but rather will suffer with him.

Satan has two forces under his control. One of these is raw power, by which he seeks to drive people away from God and into his service. The other is his propaganda, that he and not Christ is worthy of worship. Or he may seek to use the name of Christ Himself to bring about his ends. He will often masquerade "as an angel of light" (2 Corinthians 11:14) as he uses his own false teachings to deceive people, turn them away from the truth, and lead them to destruction.

In the visions presented in this week's lessons, the cosmic struggle between God and Satan for God's elect comes to the forefront.

1 The Dragon—Satan (Revelation 12)

This set of seven visions begins with a vision in the heavens of a woman clothed in the sun and of a dragon. The woman is about to give birth, and the dragon waits to devour the child once he is born. After the child is born the woman goes into the wilderness for 1,260 days (three and a half years), where God takes care of her. From here the vision moves to the war in heaven, where the dragon is defeated by the hosts of God and cast down from the sky. Satan, active on earth, will seek to defeat "the rest of her offspring," who remain protected by God.

The imagery here shows the lengths to which Satan will go to destroy God's church and take God's people for himself. It is tempting to think of the woman here as the Virgin Mary, who gave birth to our Lord, who is most certainly the child portrayed in this vision. Yet, that is not the picture being presented. Since the woman wears a crown of 12 stars, the sign of the believing community, she undoubtedly represents God's faithful people. Christ, who is the Son of God and the Son of Mary, was born out of God's believing people, those who looked for the coming of the Savior. Descended from Abraham, He was born into the very people whom He came to save.

The dragon, who is Satan (12:9), is a powerful adversary, as noted by his seven heads and 10 horns, which point to his great wisdom and power. The crowns on his head are diadems, crowns that represent deity. By wearing such crowns, he shows his own aspirations to deity, his desire to supplant God as the ruler of the universe. He waits to devour Christ and prevent Him from saving His people. We see examples of Satan's attempts to do this in the temptation accounts recorded in the Gospels. Satan used every deception he could think of to turn Christ aside from His task of redemption, tempting Him to make Himself a king without the cross.

Yet in spite of these attempts, Christ was preserved in His task, and when it was completed He was "caught up to God" (12:5), that is, He ascended into heaven. God's believing people, the church, has "fled into the wilderness" (12:6). She is in exile from her home, which is heaven. The time of this exile is 1,260 days, three and a half years. This is the time of persecution, during which God provides a place of refuge for His people, that is, keeps them under His care even in the midst of tribulation.

From here the scene switches to heaven, as Michael and his angels strive against Satan and his hosts. Satan is ultimately defeated and decisively cast from heaven. But while the victory in heaven has been won, and the eternal victory of the people of God has been accomplished "by the blood of the Lamb," Satan has not given up. He now turns his attention to earth, where he seeks to drive as many away from Christ as possible. Nevertheless, the church is saved, borne up on eagle's wings, a description God Himself used to describe His deliverance of Israel from Egypt (Exodus 19:4). The church is carried to refuge and safety during that time of persecution ("time, and times, and half a time"; namely three and a half years). God's elect remain under His protection no matter how fierce the attacks of Satan become. Though Satan may even send out a flood against the people of God, whether it be physical or spiritual, God will see that that flood is swallowed up. Unable to destroy the believing community as a whole, Satan turns his attention to the rest of her offspring—individual believers, those who joyfully keep God's commands and testify of Jesus—and seeks to destroy them one by one.

2 The First Beast—Anti-Christian World Powers (Revelation 13:1–10)

In order to bring individuals to their downfall, Satan makes use of the two beasts under his control. As the dragon, Satan, stands by the sea, he summons forth the first beast, who, like the dragon, has seven heads and 10 horns, and the crowns that he is wearing are diadems. From John's perspective, he is looking west over the sea, in the direction of Rome, as the beast rises from the sea. For John's first readers, the anti-Christian world power that they were forced to contend with was Rome itself, whose head, the emperor, had aspirations to deity.

Rome, of course, was not the last empire to wage war against the people of God. People in every age have had to suffer such warfare, whether the empire be pagan Rome, the communist Soviet Union, or militant Islamists in the Middle East. When one such empire falls, another always seems to rise to take its place. That amazing resiliency is seen in the beast's fatal wound, which has healed. The beast that John sees shows that the same anti-Christian power will be at work until God brings this age to its close. As God gave "all authority in heaven and on earth" to Christ (Matthew 28:18), so Satan gives all of his authority to the beast. This beast blatantly blasphemes God, defying God and His people by bringing disgrace upon God and bringing death to God's people.

When the world sees the strength of this beast and compares it to the weakness perceived in the people of God, the people of the world know whom they want to support. People are attracted to power, and the great power of this beast will cause all of the inhabitants of the earth—that is, all those whose names are not written in the Book of Life—to worship it. In fact, when God's people see the seeming omnipotence of the beast, they themselves may be tempted to give up and join in that chorus of praise. Yet, while the beast exercises authority for 42 months (again, three and a half years, a period of time limited by God), God's people, being forewarned and thus forearmed, know that faithful endurance amid the harshest persecution will result in eternal life.

3 The Second Beast—Anti-Christian Propaganda (Revelation 13:11–18)

The second beast that exercises authority over the earth on Satan's behalf comes out of the earth. This beast is Satan's anti-Christian propaganda. Looking toward the land, John would be facing the province of Asia, where the cult of emperor worship, the fulfillment of these words in John's own age, was quite powerful. This beast has two horns like a lamb, but it speaks like a dragon (13:11); that is, he masquerades as Christ, but his words are in fact the words of Satan. His purpose is to make the earth and its inhabitants worship the first beast. Thus he functions as an anti-Spirit. He works through the use of false miracles. These counterfeit miracles are imitations of true miracles performed by God's prophets, such as calling down fire from heaven as Elijah did on Mount Carmel.

That fire from heaven forced the prophets of Baal to acknowledge the Lord as God. These false signs deceive the inhabitants of the earth into worshiping the first beast, the false Christ who seemed to be fatally wounded but yet lived. Note that the ones deceived are "those who dwell on earth," not the elect. Try as he will, Satan will not be able to deceive God's elect. Christ has assured us of that (Matthew 24:24).

Those whom the beast cannot convert he will seek to destroy. By the breath of Satan's propaganda, the first beast, who exercises Satan's power, will order the deaths of those who refuse to worship him. To separate his people from the rest, the beast forces a mark upon all of his followers, a mockery of the seal God has put on his people—the sign of the cross. As God's people bear the name of Christ, so the worshipers of the beast bear his name and number.

The number of the beast is given as 666. The number six may be understood as a falling short of perfection, one less than perfect seven. As 777 would express the perfection of the Trinity, 666 would express the falling short of perfection of the anti-Trinity.

Those who do not possess the "mark of the beast" will not be able to buy or sell without that mark. Those who are opposed to Christ will use all the force at their disposal to make life difficult for God's people, including starving them. Throughout the ages, both the civil and ecclesiastical governments opposed to the Gospel—and sometimes in alliance with one another—have brought economic sanctions against God's people, from pagan Rome with the seal or stamp of the emperor, to ecclesiastical Rome, to the Islamic Turks in their conquest of Christian lands, to communist governments that have demanded party membership and thus renunciation of Christ for those who desire the best jobs.

Does "666" predict the modern electronic era in which the government has all sorts of information about individuals? Is the "mark of the beast" an electronic banking number that may even contain the number 666? Such an interpretation, of course, is erroneous, since the signs of the end are visible in every age. At the same time, we need to recognize that Satan can and will use any and every means available to complete his task. While electronic banking systems are morally neutral and are not being predicted here, anti-Christian governments can use them for their own purposes, as they can use anything else. The words are given to us to remind us not of the dangers of the electronic age, but of the fact that being a child of God in this world may bring hardship.

There is no theology of glory, no assurance that life in this world will always go well for the child of God here. Rather, there are times when God's people will suffer for their faith. God does not promise deliverance from such trials. He does promise to bring us through them to Himself.

4 God's Victory Assured (Revelation 14:1–13)

The scene shifts from an earth in which the agents of Satan are triumphant to Mount Zion, the heavenly Jerusalem, where Jesus stands with the 144,000, the totality of His people. These are those who had the seal of Christ on their foreheads rather than the mark of the beast. Rather than being devoted to evil, they are "blameless." Their sins have been covered by the blood of Christ, and, having come through death, they now stand spotless before God (Ephesians 5:27; Jude 24).

The voice "like the roar of many waters" they hear is like the voice of Christ described in 1:15 and 4:5, and they themselves sing a "new song" before the reference to the frequent invitation recorded in the Psalms (Psalm 98:1; 144:9; 149:1). Since it is sung to the King of heaven rather than to the ruler of this world it can only be sung by the people of God.

They are described as pure, for they have not committed spiritual adultery by going after false gods or by defiling themselves by indulging in the practices of the surrounding society. Rather than following the world, they have heeded Christ's command, "Follow Me!" As the choicest produce was offered to God in the Old Testament, so God's children are offered to Him as firstfruits, purchased by Christ Himself.

The scene now shifts away from heaven and back to earth. Though the visions concerning the beasts show the world as under the control of Satan's agents, we now see three angels and hear that the destiny of the world is ultimately in God's hands.

The message of the first angel is a call to the world to repent and to turn to the true God. As long as this age endures that message will not be silenced, and God will continue to call people out of the world to Himself.

The second angel calls out, "Fallen is Babylon the great." The anti-Christian powers of the world will meet their doom. Babylon, the great military power of the sixth century before Christ, had invaded Jerusalem, destroyed the temple, and deposed the king. It seemed as though Israel was destroyed forever. Demanding the worship of its own gods, Babylon threatened the faithful with death, even in a fiery furnace (Daniel 3). Yet within 70 years Babylon itself had fallen and Israel was restored to its land.

Now Rome was doing the same. Israel had been conquered, and in AD 70 the temple was again destroyed. Now emperor worship was being imposed upon God's people. The similarity of Rome to Babylon was so great that Babylon had become a code word for Rome among Christians (1 Peter 5:13). But the cry of the angel declares that even now Babylon is as good as destroyed, for the victory belongs to God. All of the powers exemplified by Babylon will ultimately be destroyed.

The message of the third angel speaks to those who listen to the message coming out of Babylon: Those who worship the beast will eventually drink the wine of God's fury. Here the frightening, and very real, specter of eternal punishment for the wicked is proclaimed. This is not done in a triumphant manner. There is no rejoicing in the punishments of the wicked by a self-congratulatory group that has managed to escape. Rather it is a solemn warning to the world that God is not mocked and that evil will be punished.

It also serves as an admonition to the people of God to endure to the end and to remain faithful. For those who do, the voice from heaven declares, "Blessed are the dead who die in the Lord." This is the second of the seven beatitudes recorded in Revelation. The dead in Christ will enter the rest that God has promised for His people, their works following them, giving evidence of their faithfulness.

5 The Final Harvest (Revelation 14:14–20)

Ultimately, the end will come. Christ will return, wearing the crown of His kingship, declaring His sovereignty to all the world, and carrying the sickle that will inaugurate the harvest. When Christ has harvested His own, the angels under Him will harvest the rest of the world, pouring them into the "winepress of the wrath of God," an image taken from the Old Testament (Isaiah 63:3; Lamentations 1:15; Joel 3:13), where the execution of God's wrath is compared to the treading of grapes. The number 1,600 is four (the number of the world) multiplied by itself, then multiplied twice by 10, the number of completeness, showing the finality of God's judgment on the earth. Sixteen hundred stadia is the approximate length of Palestine from north to south, the massive outflowing of blood showing the extent of God's judgment against the wickedness of the world.

What does this series of visions have to say to us? As powerful as Satan seems to be, the strong one will be overcome by One who is stronger—Christ Himself. Satan, his power, and his propaganda—Anti-God, Antichrist, and Anti-Spirit—will all be destroyed in the end, as will all of those who have followed them. God's people, forced to suffer and even die for their commitment to Christ, will emerge victorious, singing the eternal new song before the throne of God forever.

Concluding Activities

If time permits, dismiss the group with an affirmation of trust in God by reading Psalm 46:1–7. Then distribute study leaflet 6 after making any necessary announcements.

Praise for God and Armageddon for the World

Revelation 15–16

Preparing for the Session

Central Focus

This week we see that the world stands under God's curse because of its rebellion against Him; but for God's people even the worst of events can bring a blessing. God is always in control. Even in the midst of persecution and tribulation He will cause blessings to result, and thus He deserves our constant praise. The people of the world fail to realize this and will suffer judgment and destruction.

Objectives

That participants, led by the Holy Spirit, will

1. see the reality of God's judgment upon the world;
2. rejoice in the victory that Christ has won over the world; and
3. praise God for revealing that victory to His own.

Note for the small-group leaders: Lesson notes and other materials you will need begin on page 70.

For the Lecture Leader

Session Plan

Worship

Begin the session with the hymn printed in the study leaflet. Accompaniments are available in denominational hymnals, such as *Lutheran Service Book* or *Lutheran Worship* (refer to hymnal index). (Note: Concordia Publishing House has available *The Concordia Organist.* All the initial worship hymns in the LifeLight courses are included in this resource. It's especially helpful for mission congregations and small parishes. See the list of study resources on page 7.)

Prayer

Lord God, You are majestic and marvelous in Your providential guidance of Your people. With Moses we sing our anthem of praise, "Great and amazing are Your deeds, O Lord God the Almighty! Just and true are Your ways, O King of the nations! Who will not fear, O Lord, and glorify Your name? For You alone are holy." Yet the people of the world continue to curse and mock You. Reveal both Your judgment upon their sin but also Your readiness to forgive because of Your mercy and love in Christ Jesus. Amen.

Lecture Presentation

Introduction

We have seen in past lessons how God uses the various powers of the world to call attention to His judgment—the evil results of sin, the forces of nature, even false religious teachings that must ultimately show the futility of trusting in ourselves. We have seen how Satan, unable to destroy the church as a whole, seeks to deceive and oppress individual believers with his power and propaganda, and how the world gladly does Satan's bidding, being more intrigued by the power of Satan than by the grace of God. Nevertheless, we have also seen that God will bring His people to victory through all of this, because the Lamb has already won the victory.

We need to remember all of this as we move on to the next set of visions, that of the seven last plagues, the seven bowls of the wrath of God.

Once again it is important to remember that the events described here cover the entire New Testament era, from Christ's ascension until His return. The focus, however, now turns specifically to the wrath of God, His holy and righteous anger against a disobedient and disbelieving humanity.

All signs of God's judgment against the world, and especially the idea of His wrath, do not sit well with the people of this supposedly enlightened age. The very idea that God is a God of wrath is an affront to modern sensibilities. Such an attribute is considered to be incompatible with the idea of a loving God. A loving God, many think, would forgive without the shedding of blood and without repentance on the part of the sinner; most certainly He would never punish people for eternity!

Yet, a little further thought shows us that this could not be the case. True love, which desires the best for humanity, cannot tolerate evil, which by its very nature runs roughshod over anything that stands in the way of one's own desires. God, being *both holy and loving,* takes sin seriously. The wrath of God therefore does not contradict His love but is entirely consistent with it. It is true that God does not desire the death of the wicked, but those who refuse to repent of their wickedness must face God's wrath against them. It has been said, "God hates the sin but loves the sinner." Yet, while God has indeed shown love for all sinners, sin and the sinner cannot be easily separated. The sinner who refuses to repent will be held accountable. We must remember that it is not people's sins that make them sinners. Rather, people sin because they are sinners. Christ Himself pointed out that sin comes out of the human heart (Mark 7:20–23), a heart that is naturally corrupt.

Nevertheless, God showed His love for us *because "while we were still sinners,* Christ died for us" (Romans 5:8), that is for the whole of humanity. The love of God is manifested not by ignoring evil, but by pouring out His wrath against evil upon His Son rather than upon us who deserve it. Only through repentance and faith in Christ can a distinction be made between the sin and the one who sins. Only because we are a "new creation" (2 Corinthians 5:17) can we say, "It is no longer I who do it [evil], but sin that dwells within me" (Romans 7:17). As for those who refuse to repent but instead prefer to wallow in their evil, God's Word is clear: The wrath of God remains upon them (John 3:36). The bowls of God's wrath, then, are not poured out upon the whole of humanity, but only upon the unrighteous, for the sins of God's people are covered by the blood of the Lamb. The tragedy is that Christ died even for those who reject Him. It is by their own choice that they receive wrath rather than glory.

1 Appearance of the Seven Angels (Revelation 15)

As with the visions of the seals and trumpets, the scene begins in heaven as preparations are made for the pouring out of the seven last plagues, which complete the wrath of God. These plagues affect not just one fourth or one third of the earth, but the entire earth. Once again, the people of God who have come through the great tribulation, described as "those who had conquered the beast," stand at the sea of glass (see 4:6), now perceived as being mixed with fire, reflecting the glory of God, before whose throne they stand. Their victory over the beast looks to the world like defeat, for they won that victory by dying. Thus they followed the example of the Lamb, whose death is the source of their victory and whose resurrection made that victory apparent. They trusted the word of Christ, who assured them that they need not fear anyone who could kill the body but could not kill the soul (Matthew 10:28).

Verse 3—The song the saints sing is described as "the song of Moses, the servant of God, and the song of the Lamb." The Old Testament describes two songs of Moses: The first, recorded in Exodus 15:1–18, was sung after God brought Israel through the Red Sea. The second, recorded in Deuteronomy 32, was sung at the close of Moses' farewell speech to Israel, just before his death and just before Israel entered into the Promised Land. Both songs declare God's power and God's sovereignty over history and declare God's victory over His enemies. Both declare that in the end all nations will recognize that the Lord is God.

These themes are echoed in the words recorded in this chapter. The words "Great and amazing are Your deeds," summarize the themes of many of the psalms and other songs of the Old Testament, which give glory to God by listing His mighty acts on behalf of His people.

But the song they sing is also the "song of the Lamb." As Moses was the first deliverer of Israel, leading them to the Promised Land, so the Lamb, the last deliverer, through His death and resurrection, has led His people to eternal life. The song sung by Moses proclaimed the deliverance that established the people of God as a nation. The song of the Lamb, sung to the Lamb and about the Lamb, proclaims the eternal deliverance of God's people from all of their enemies, including death itself. By His continued preservation of His people and by His mighty acts, God shows Himself to be truly the King of the Ages.

Verses 5–6—Once again the temple in heaven, the tabernacle of the Testimony, is opened, and the seven angels with the seven plagues come out. Dressed in linen and wearing golden sashes, they show that they are exercising priestly functions to the world. They serve as mediators of God's punishment to the world. In the previous lesson, the three angels announced the everlasting Gospel and announced God's judgment upon the world. Now what has been announced will be enacted, as that judgment is carried out, as the angels receive the bowls containing the plagues from one of the four living creatures.

As the tabernacle in the wilderness and the temple in Jerusalem served to point to the presence of God among His people in the Old Testament, so does the heavenly temple here. The smoke, which is the glory of God, appears, making God's presence among His people known as it did in the Old Testament—in the tabernacle (Exodus 40:34), in the temple from the very day of its dedication (1 Kings 8:10–11), to Isaiah the prophet, who saw God's presence in the heavenly temple as he was called to service (Isaiah 6:1–8). Verse 8—Since no sinful human can see God and live, and since no one can stand under the righteous wrath of the most holy God, no one is allowed in the temple until the pouring out of God's wrath is completed.

2 The Seven Bowls of Wrath (Revelation 16)

The angels are then sent out to pour the bowls of God's wrath out upon the earth. The plagues that are poured out have parallels with the plagues associated with the seven trumpets, which in turn had parallels with the plagues God visited upon the Egyptians. As the plagues against the Egyptians showed God's judgment against an unbelieving people who had enslaved God's people, so the plagues of the seven bowls are directed exclusively against the unbelieving of the world. They do not affect the people of God.

This does not mean that the church has been "raptured" out of the world before the plagues are sent. As with the previous visions, the events described take place throughout the age of the church. The plagues mentioned are sent both to drive people to repentance, as the experience of God's wrath may do in this life (though that wrath cannot convert anyone—only the Good News of Christ can do that) and ultimately to punish those who refuse to repent.

Verse 2—The first bowl is poured out on the land, just as the first trumpet affected the land. The result: Sores break out on the people who worshiped the beast and had his mark upon them. The description is reminiscent of the sixth plague poured out on Egypt, in which boils and abscesses broke out upon the people. In Egypt God was forced to use such drastic measures because, in spite of the clear evidence that Moses was speaking for God, Pharaoh refused to listen. Those who followed Pharaoh, who bore his stamp, were the recipients of the plague. So also those who bear the stamp of the beast will receive the brunt of this plague. Speaking in spiritual terms, those who follow the beast and worship his power will in the end find that their hopes are fruitless and their spirits in agony as they realize that the powers of this world will pass away and only God and His own endure forever.

The second plague affects the waters of the sea. The third plague affects the waters of the land—rivers and springs—as did the third trumpet. In both cases, the waters turn to blood, as did the waters of the Nile in the first of the plagues with which the Lord struck Egypt (Exodus 7:14–24). The result is death—death to every living thing in the sea and death to those who have put God's people to death.

Verse 5—The angel in charge of the waters notes the justice of God's judgment as he tailors the punishment to fit the crime. Verse 6—Those who have shed the blood of the saints are now forced to drink blood. The irony of this situation must not be lost. The shedding of blood is a most holy act in the eyes of God, for without the shedding of blood there is no forgiveness of sins (Hebrews 9:22). Throughout the Old Testament, God required blood sacrifices as a type, or foreshadowing, of the great sacrifice that was to come—the sacrifice of His only Son, who shed His blood once for all of humanity. Rejecting the blood of Christ, they instead shed the blood of His servants, some in complete, knowing rebellion against God, others thinking that by doing so they are doing God a favor. So instead of drinking the blood of Christ in the cup of blessing given in the Sacrament of the Altar, the very blood poured out for them, they are forced to drink the blood of God's wrath that runs through the rivers of the land.

Verse 8—The fourth bowl is poured out on the sun, as the fourth trumpet struck the heavens. The sun then sends forth its fire to strike the people. While the end is not yet, and these fires are not yet the fires of eternal punishment, they are a foretaste of that punishment. God destroyed Sodom and Gomorrah with fire and brimstone because of their wickedness. Moses, in the blessings and curses pronounced in his farewell speech, announced the curse of scorching heat upon those who would not obey God (Deuteronomy 28:22). At the end of the world the universe itself will be consumed in flames (2 Peter 3:7) and the works of every human being will be tested in the fires of God's judgment (1 Corinthians 3:13); only those works done for Christ in faith will survive.

Verse 9—This being not the final judgment, one of the

purposes is still to bring people to repentance, but it will not have that effect. Rather than acknowledging error, human self-righteousness defies God to the end, preferring punishment to admission of wrongdoing. In fact, now they are more than merely impenitent. Knowing that it is God who is striking them they turn and blaspheme God for giving them what they deserve.

Verse 10—The fifth angel pours out his bowl on the throne of the beast and plunges it into darkness. Even before this age comes to an end, the agents of Satan will be shown to be powerless. Though thought to be the one who offers all of the blessings of power and prosperity, Satan's throne will be plunged into darkness, and his followers will as well. The euphoria of following the beast is only temporary. Just as the drug-induced "high" creates an artificial sense of well-being that must ultimately give way to depression as it wears off, so also the artificial "high" gained by following the beast, the giddiness of being associated with power, must ultimately give way to despair as his followers realize that the one who is really in charge has dethroned the beast, and they have nothing left for themselves but the pain of the "darkness," a sense of abandonment and utter hopelessness.

Verse 11—Yet they will still refuse to repent, even in the midst of their pain. Pride refuses to humble itself, even in the face of the obvious. Just as Pharaoh and his priests, when confronted with the ninth plague, the plague of darkness, refused to listen to Moses, so these people will refuse to listen.

Verse 12—The angel with the sixth bowl pours it out on the Euphrates, the river that marks the traditional eastern boundary between the lands of the Gentiles and the Promised Land (Genesis 15:18; Deuteronomy 1:7). Historically, the nations of the East were the traditional enemies of the people of God—the ones who sought to destroy the nation completely: Assyria, Babylon, Persia. The invasion now is a spiritual invasion; demonic spirits looking like frogs (listed among the unclean animals for the Jews in Leviticus 11:10) come out of the mouths of the beasts and the dragon. Speaking their lying words and performing their lying wonders, they entice the kings of the world to do battle against the people of God. In spite of all they have seen, the enemies of God's people still believe victory is possible and gather *en masse* for one final conflict.

Yet the very forces that seek to destroy the people of God will be used by God to bring about their own destruction. Gathering together for battle, they expect to destroy, but that battle will in fact inaugurate their own end. The time here is the "little while" that will be mentioned in 20:3. Satan, loosed from his chains, again will be seeking to deceive the nations, in his pride failing to realize that the battle he initiates will bring about his own destruction.

Verse 15—Here Christ warns His people that, though He will win the battle, His own people need to be prepared. The same language was used by Christ while on earth, as He prepared His disciples for the last days. He warns them that the tribulation will reach its worst shortly before the end, but that He will shorten the days of tribulation by His return, which will be as unexpected as a thief (Matthew 24:43). Taking a cue from Christ's illustration, St. Paul also declares that Christ will return "like a thief in the night" (1 Thessalonians 5:2), and thus both Jesus and Paul exhorted the people of God to stay awake, prepared at all times. Jesus warns His people to be prepared to flee the invasion to come, using the forthcoming battle, which would lead to the destruction of Jerusalem, as a foreshadowing of the great spiritual battle for human souls as the age draws to a close. Those not prepared will be exposed to destruction, but those who keep watch and are prepared for the end are called "blessed." This is the third beatitude.

Verse 16—The place of this great spiritual battle is named Armageddon. The name, found nowhere else in Scripture, means "Mountain of Megiddo." The Plain of Megiddo was a significant strategic site in Israel (the Northern Kingdom after the monarchy was divided after the death of Solomon). Though there is no specific mountain by that name, one of the most significant mountains in that region is Mount Carmel, the mountain where God through Elijah defeated the priests of Baal. Brought there for battle against the forces of Baal, Elijah stood alone, and by God's direct act of sending fire from heaven, he prevailed. Armageddon is clearly a spiritual battle, in which the enemies of God gather against His people for the final confrontation, at which time God intervenes directly to bring about the destruction of His enemies.

That destruction takes place as the seventh bowl is poured out. The voice from the throne then thunders, "It is done!" and God makes His presence known. The lightning, thunder, and earthquakes that always signal the presence of the majesty of God occur once again, as they had at Mount Sinai. But while at Sinai they announced the covenant, at Armageddon they announce judgment. While Christ noted that earthquakes, in general, serve as a sign of the end (Matthew 24:7), such an earthquake as this had never occurred before. For this earthquake brings about the destruction of Babylon itself and of all of the cities of the nations. As God used hail to destroy his enemies in the past, going before Joshua and the Israelite army at Gibeon, (Joshua 10:10–11), so He will do so at the end. God will unleash His full fury upon the world, and the result will be its total destruction.

Some popular books dealing with the end times treat all of the events mentioned here, including the battle of Armageddon, as literal, physical events that will happen immediately before the end. They go so far as to say that the things described are such that they could not have occurred until the present era. According to these books, Revelation supposedly predicts the development of electronic banking, the fires of nuclear war, the rise to prominence of the European Economic Community in the first beast, and so forth.

Such interpretations go contrary to the tenor of the entire Book of Revelation, which quite clearly declares itself to be symbolic. To become preoccupied with timetables concerning the events of the end distracts us from remembering the true purpose of the signs—to remind Christians in all ages that Christ is coming soon. The signs are there to point out that Christ's coming is imminent, and that it has been ever since the day He ascended to the Father.

Revelation was not written 2,000 years ago in order to be a hidden book whose meaning can only be deciphered today. It was written to help Christians in all ages to put their trust in Christ even in the worst of times. Whenever they see these signs they can be assured that this world and its trials will not last, but that Christ is going to return. Thus even in the midst of their troubles they can sing their praises to God.

Nor does the fact that the bowls of wrath do not fall upon members of the church mean that the church is no longer on earth during that time. Some have suggested that the church will be "raptured" from the world before God's wrath is poured out, and that this wrath is the great tribulation poured out against the world. During that time, these people say that more believers, the "great multitude that no one could number" (Revelation 7:9), will be converted, and that these will be "the ones coming out of the great tribulation" (7:14), in distinction from the church, which will already be in heaven. The "blessed hope" promised by St. Paul (Titus 2:13) then becomes the rapture of the church rather than what it really is—eternal life.

The most insidious danger associated with that view is the notion that there will be a second chance for people who do not believe now—that they have time to repent before the end after Christ comes back for His church. Such incorrect ideas must be rejected, for they come from taking a symbolic book and reading it in a literalistic manner, and then reading their conclusions back into the rest of the Scriptures. Far from being a "Grand Central Station" in which all the threads of prophecy come together and are finally understood, Revelation is a book written in such a manner that only knowledge of the rest of the Scriptures makes proper interpretation possible. Rather than detailing a complex series of events the sole purpose of which is to show God's glory by their fulfillment, the book restates the simple message that Christ is with His people even to the end of the age and that the victory has already been won. God's people will be saved—this evil world will be destroyed. Praise God that it is all in His hands and that we have eternal life assured!

Concluding Activities

Close this week of praise for God with the best-known English song of praise, the Common Doxology, which was written some 300 years ago by Bishop Thomas Ken. Catch its inclusiveness as you sing and pray it.

> Praise God, from whom all blessings flow;
> Praise Him, all creatures here below;
> Praise Him above, O heaven'ly host;
> Praise Father, Son, and Holy Ghost.

The Agony of the Wicked and the Ecstasy of the Saved

Revelation 17–19

Preparing for the Session

Central Focus

Satan seduces the people of this world, luring them into idolatry and service to him in his goal of destroying the church. But God shows us that these seductive powers will be destroyed along with the Antichrist's power and propaganda. God's people will triumph victoriously and celebrate joyously their marriage to the Lamb.

Objectives

That participants, led by the Holy Spirit, will

1. realize that Satan's efforts to seduce the world are doomed to destruction, as are his Antichrist power and propaganda;
2. rejoice to see Christ preserve His own, while Satan and his helpers are destroyed; and
3. see the seductive ungodliness of this world slain by Him who sat upon the white horse and now is crowned King of Kings and Lord of Lords.

Note for the small-group leaders: Lesson notes and other materials you will need begin on page 72.

For the Lecture Leader

Session Plan

Worship

Begin the session with the hymn printed in the study leaflet. Accompaniments are available in denominational hymnals, such as *Lutheran Service Book* or *Lutheran Worship* (refer to hymnal index). (Note: Concordia Publishing House has available *The Concordia Organist*. All the initial worship hymns in the LifeLight courses are included in this resource. It's especially helpful for mission congregations and small parishes. See the list of study resources on page 7.)

Pray together the prayer printed in the study leaflet.

Lecture Presentation

Introduction

The present age will be brought to an end when God cries "It is done!" from His heavenly throne and pours out His wrath upon the world. The vision of the seven bowls showed the outpouring of God's wrath upon those who followed the beast, that is, upon rebellious humanity. Attention now turns to the destruction of Satan's agents, the two beasts, the Antichrist and Anti-Spirit, Satan's power and propaganda. The vision of the destruction of the beasts and the fall of Babylon, which causes great agony for the people of this world who attached themselves to her, is followed by another glimpse of heaven, where the saints of God utter ecstatic cries of praise to God for His salvation as they celebrate the wedding supper of the Lamb.

1 A Woman Sitting on a Beast (Revelation 17)

Verses 1–4—The seventh bowl has begun the description of the final judgment, noting the reaction of the people of the world—the inhabitants of the earth—to God's judgment against them: rage and cursing against God. Now one of the angels who poured out the bowls of wrath upon the world comes to John specifically to show him the judgment of God against Babylon—the anti-church who seeks to draw the saints from God to herself. She is named Babylon, and like the historical city of Babylon, she sits upon "many waters" (Jeremiah 51:13), though the waters here represent all peoples, multitudes, nations, and languages (Revelation 17:15), rather than the Euphrates River and the elaborate network of irrigation canals that marked the historical city. Like historical Babylon, this Babylon is also a "great city" (Revelation 17:18), so large that it dwarfs the comparative few who are God's chosen.

The woman who is Babylon is in every way the opposite of the woman clothed with the sun, described in chapter 12. She is portrayed as a prostitute seated upon the beast from the sea—the Antichrist, Satan's anti-Christian power. She is called the great prostitute—classic language called her "the whore of Babylon"—because she entices humanity away from faithfulness to the true God to go lusting after herself.

The rulers of the world ally themselves with her ("have committed sexual immorality") because in their eyes she has more to offer than God Himself does. She creates the illusion that her pleasures are greater than God's pleasures, for in this world the people of God bear crosses rather than crowns. Failing to see the crown promised in the next life, they strive to receive a crown of glory for accomplishments in this life, not realizing that such a crown will wither and fade, as do all the treasures of this world.

Clothed in the riches of this world, she despises those who are clothed from above with the righteousness of Christ. Instead of the cup of blessing inaugurated by Christ, she holds the cup of abominations that she offers to her own followers. Verse 6—Indeed, the anti-church that deceives the world has herself become drunk with the blood of the saints, gleefully putting to death the faithful while exalting herself. Making herself alluring to the world, she is in fact an abomination in the eyes of God and His people.

In the Old Testament the intimate relationship between God and His people is often compared to that of a husband and wife, and in the New Testament the imagery is transformed to show the relationship between Christ and His church. Jesus often refers to Himself as the Bridegroom, and Paul makes much of the comparison in Ephesians 5:22–33. The image of Christ as the Bridegroom and the church as His bride will be continued in the vision of the marriage supper of the Lamb (Revelation 19:6–10).

The relationship between Christ and His church has been called a mystery (Ephesians 5:32), and Christ's servants have been called "stewards of the mysteries of God" (1 Corinthians 4:1), those formerly hidden things that God has now revealed to His people. Verse 5—The great prostitute also bears a title of Mystery on her forehead. As the servants of Christ are marked on their foreheads with the seal of Christ, and as the servants of the beast are marked with his seal, so also the anti-church is branded as such. Claiming for herself an attribute of the true church, her mysteries in fact lead to destruction rather than salvation.

Verse 8—The beast, on which the great prostitute sits, is the Antichrist, the one, who in imitation of the Lamb, is described as the one who "was and is not and is to come" (17:8), just as the Lamb who once was dead now lives (1:18; 2:8). He comes from out of the bottomless pit, the realm of Satan himself. The beast is described in terms of his activity in human history, as he continually works through the nations of the world to oppress God's people.

Verses 9–10—The description of the sevenfold kingdom may be a reference to the six great empires of the ancient world, from Egypt through Rome, the one who "now is," and with the seventh yet to come, who would endure for a little while, being all anti-Christian powers in the subsequent times. There will always be such kings in the world who will seek to destroy the church. Verse 11—The eighth is the beast himself, who is the power behind the empires, the one who exercises the power of Satan to attack God's people in every generation. Though enduring through the ages of this world, he, too, is going to his destruction.

Verse 12—Who are the 10 kings to come? Ten is the number of completeness; therefore the number refers to all future kings of this world who ally themselves with the power of the Antichrist. They will endure for an hour, that is, like all earthly realms, they will last but a short time, and they, too, will be destroyed. The only kingdom that will endure will be the kingdom of our Lord and of His Christ. And He shall reign forever and ever.

Verse 16—Though the anti-church sits upon the Antichrist, and through him exercises power over the kings of the earth, the unholy alliance between the anti-church and Satan's power cannot endure. Just as a wild horse will tolerate a rider while he must, but will throw him off at the first opportunity, so the beast will throw off the control of the anti-church when the opportunity arises. Ultimately, Babylon will be destroyed by the beast, who unwittingly serves as an agent of God's judgment.

2 The Fall of Babylon (Revelation 18)

The historical city of Babylon, which oppressed the people of God and took them into captivity and exile, is the reference point for the Babylon of Revelation. Just as the prophets Isaiah (Isaiah 21:9) and Jeremiah (Jeremiah 51:8) prophesied the fall of Babylon while she was still in the midst of her glory, so also the angel of Revelation 18:1–3 announces the fall of Babylon (the devil and his followers) while John and his readers (including us!) find spiritual Babylon still at the height of her powers. But the word of the angel is certain: just as historical Babylon fell, never to rise again (Jeremiah 51:64), so also spiritual Babylon must ultimately fall and never rise again. Chapter 18 describes the fall from its announcement, to the reaction of the world, to the results and implications of that fall.

The angel who announces the fall of Babylon describes the city as she really is—a haunt for evil and for everything detestable. In spite of what she is by nature, indeed even because of it, the nations of the world, the kings, and the merchants were enamored with her, because she gave them what they wanted. Verse 4—The people of God, who must live among her, are called upon by the voice of Christ Himself to come out of her, just as Lot and his family were called upon to leave Sodom and never to look back, so that they might escape the destruction that the city deserves.

What the city deserves she will get. "Vengeance is mine!" the Lord cries (Deuteronomy 32:35; Romans 12:19), and He gives back to Babylon everything that she has dished out upon His people. Verse 6—She will be paid back double for her evil, as will all who once knew God but turned away, and she will be forced to drink from the cup of her own abominations, to reap the consequences of her own actions. In her own pride she sees herself as invincible, totally in control. Such pride can only end with destruction. She who exalts herself to the heavens will be brought to destruction by God Himself.

Those who closely attached themselves to Babylon will see her destruction and be terrified by it. The words of the lament are closely patterned on the words of Ezekiel 27, as the prophet laments over the city of Tyre. Three groups are mentioned here—kings, merchants, and seamen. But the words they issue are words eulogizing the city for what it was and lamenting its destruction. There is not a shred of penitence among them, nor is there any mention of the evils perpetrated by that city. Having had a part in the city and having partaken in her pleasures, a religion that made them feel good and gave them what they wanted, these people lament its destruction because it means an end to their own wealth and well-being and because it is a prelude to their own destruction.

Verses 9–10—The kings who committed adultery with her, who lay in the lap of her luxury, weep and mourn at the suddenness of her doom. Verses 11–17—The merchants of the world lament the fact that the destruction of the city means that no one is left to buy their precious cargoes. At the height of Babylon's power, no one who did not bear the mark of the beast could buy or sell. Now she who poured out her wrath on God's people finds herself the recipient of God's wrath, and those that profited from her luxury are themselves left destitute. She who had the wealth of the world is brought to ruin in but an hour.

Verses 18–19—So also those who make their living from the sea, who deliver the cargo of the merchants. They, too, cry out in lament at the destruction of the great city, for they had become rich because of her wealth, and now she is ruined. They throw dust on their heads in lamentation, but not in repentance. Their sorrow is not over the evil in which they had a part but in the loss of the power they once had through her.

Verse 20—In counterpoint to the words of those who lament the fall of Babylon, the angel narrating these events calls upon heaven and all of God's people on earth and heaven—saints, apostles, and prophets, to rejoice at the fall of Babylon, because God has now vindicated them. As for the servants of Babylon, they find themselves on the outside, where there is only wailing and gnashing of teeth.

Verses 21–24—To conclude the scene, another angel appears and throws a millstone into the sea, declaring that Babylon will be cast down with violence. Evil rots away the inside of those who perpetrate it, leaving only a shell that must eventually collapse of its own accord. But the destruction of Babylon comes about not because of its inherent rot, but because of the violence of God's wrath.

Looked at from one aspect, the words of the angel seem like words of lament similar to those of the kings, merchants, and seamen (and are reminiscent of Jeremiah's lament over Jerusalem [Jeremiah 25:10]), but ultimately they are words of exultation that a city responsible for the deaths of so many of God's people has been so thoroughly destroyed that it will never rise again. Yet, while there is exultation, there is no gloating.

3 Rejoicing in Heaven (Revelation 19:1–10)

Having been called upon to rejoice (Revelation 18:20), heaven responds with rejoicing, with shouts of "Hallelujah!" (The word *Hallelujah* occurs only four times in the New Testament, all of them in Revelation 19:1–6. The word is a combination of two Hebrew words that occur frequently in the Psalms, meaning "Praise the Lord!") God is praised for all that is His—all salvation, glory, and power. God has provided the victory over sin and evil; He alone possesses true majesty of His own; and He alone has the strength to subdue all of His enemies. All of these He shows as He judges all of creation and condemns the great prostitute.

Verses 1–3—The cry of the martyrs for vindication, issued in Revelation 6:9–11, has finally been answered, and God's people have been avenged. The anti-church, claiming divine prerogatives, had put God's people to death while exalting herself. Now she herself has been condemned, sent to that place where the smoke of her destruction will last forever.

Verses 4—To the cry of this multitude that no one can number, the 24 elders (the church as a whole) and the four living creatures (all of creation) respond, "Amen, Hallelujah!" That well-known Hebrew word *Amen* simply means "Yes, it is true." It is a cry of affirmation that everything proclaimed by the multitude is true. To that affirmation they add their own word of praise.

Verses 5–6—The voice from the throne then calls upon the multitude to expand upon that song of praise, calling them "His servants," and including both the small and the great. All of the people of God, from the great saints such as the apostles and prophets, down to the least, including the littlest of children and those who died as "infants in Christ" (1 Corinthians 3:1) very shortly after their conversion, like the thief of the cross, all are to join together in praise to God. To this exhortation the multitude responds with another "Hallelujah!" rejoicing that the time for the wedding of the Lamb has come.

The Bridegroom has come to take His bride into His house, where she will live with Him forever. Verses 7–8—The bride of the Lamb, which is the church, has been prepared for the wedding. She is clothed in fine linen, which we are told stands for the righteous acts of the saints. Only those who have been clothed in Christ's righteousness are able to wear such righteous acts. How different the bride is clothed, when compared to the scarlet clothes of the great prostitute! How different her deeds!

Verse 9—The angel now instructs John to write the fourth beatitude: "Blessed are those who are invited to the marriage supper of the Lamb." The picture that the Old Testament prophets used (Isaiah 54:5–7; Hosea 2:19–20) and that Christ used in His parables (Matthew 22:1–14; 25:1–13) is now being made a reality. To increase the certainty that this is the destiny of God's people, he adds the words, "These are the true words of God." John's reaction to the overwhelming joy of this promise is to fall down to worship the angel, who rightly points out that only God is worthy of such worship. As magnificent as the angels are, they themselves are but servants of God and are not worthy of the honor that is to be given to God alone. The true spirit of prophecy points to no one but Christ.

4 Final Defeat for God's Enemies (Revelation 19:11–21)

Verse 11—The one to whom all prophecy points now makes His appearance, riding a white horse. He is Christ Himself, riding out to warfare to bring His enemies down to defeat. Verse 12—Like the dragon and the beast from the sea, He, too, wears many crowns, many diadems; but unlike the dragon and the beast, He is worthy of them, for He is called Faithful and True, as He was back in Revelation 3:14. Verse 13—He wears a robe dipped in blood, showing that He goes to battle for His people, and He is known as the Word of God, as John himself noted in the first chapter of the Gospel that bears his name.

Verse 14—The armies that follow Him show that He is indeed the Lord of hosts, the Lord of armies. And the armies that follow Him are not dressed for battle; they are dressed in the garments of victory, the fine linen that is the garment of the bride of the Lamb.

Verse 15—The sword that comes from His mouth, which will strike down His enemies, is the Word of God, in this case the judgment of the Law in all of its fury. He comes as one who will rule over the nations—that is, over those of this world who would not have Him as King—with an iron scepter and will tread the winepress of God's wrath, as noted in Revelation 14:17–20. He here fulfills the words that He spoke to His disciples, which John himself recorded: "The Father . . . has given all judgment to the Son" (John 5:22).

Verse 16—The kings of the past had claimed to rule by divine right. The Roman emperor even declared himself to be lord and god. Lest anyone exalt themselves too highly, the one who rides the white horse wears His name on His robe and on His thigh: *He* is King of kings and Lord of lords. "At the name of Jesus every knee should bow" (Philippians 2:10), including the rulers of this world.

Verse 17–18—Now it is time for another supper. Those who attend the wedding supper of the Lamb are truly blessed, but those who are not part of that banquet will participate in the "great supper of God," not as guests but as the meal itself. An angel standing in the sun calls to all the birds flying in midair to the great supper, to feast on the flesh of the enemies of God. The victory of the Rider over His enemies is swift. Rather than gaining victory, they simply become carrion for the birds of prey. So it is with all who would usurp God's place and exalt themselves.

Verses 19–21—But not all of Christ's enemies are defeated yet. Those kings of the earth who had gathered together in the service of the beast (the beast from the sea) in their blind arrogance believe that it is still possible to win the victory. Their defeat is swift and sure. The account of the defeat of the kings of the earth and their armies, and of the beast and his prophet, is brief to the point of derision. Their destruction is certain, so nothing more needs to be said.

The Antichrist and the one who served him and deluded the world through false miracles are captured and thrown into the fiery lake that burns with sulfur. While the name is not used, the lake of fire is clearly *gehenna*, hell, mentioned here for the first time in Revelation. The rest of His enemies are killed, and their flesh again serves as carrion for the birds of prey. As this vision comes to an end, we again see Christ victorious and His enemies destroyed.

Conclusion

The vision began with the picture of the anti-church seated on the beast, drunk with the blood of the martyrs. It ends with the martyrs victorious and the servants of the woman and of the beast upon which she sits destroyed. The message for God's people is clear: Faithfulness will not be easy in this life, and many of God's people will be called upon to die for their faith, even at the hands of those who claim to be the church. Yet, in the end those martyrs will enjoy the blessedness of heaven with their Lord and will be guests at the wedding supper of the Lamb, while those who persecuted them will receive everything they deserve. Babylon will fall, thrown down by God. The Antichrist, Satan's power in the world, and the Anti-spirit, Satan's propaganda, seeking to conquer heaven, will be cast down into hell. Knowing this, God's people on earth can rejoice even now, knowing that their vindication is certain.

Concluding Activities

Since Revelation 19 is the only chapter in the New Testament containing the word *hallelujah,* close with the Hallelujah Psalm: 117 (the shortest chapter in the Bible).

> Praise the LORD, all nations!
> Extol Him, all peoples!
> For great is His steadfast love toward us,
> and the faithfulness of the LORD
> endures forever.
> Praise the LORD!

The Millennium and the Doom of Satan

Revelation 20

Preparing for the Session

Central Focus

In this cycle we see Satan bound for a thousand years (the millennium), during which time he will be restricted in his opposition to Christ and in his persecution of the church. Then for a final time, after the millennium, Satan will be granted opportunity for a brief period of most harsh persecution before he is cast "into the lake of fire" forever.

Objectives

That participants, led by the Holy Spirit, will

1. gain a correct understanding of the millennium;
2. grow in conviction of God's grace in Christ providing for eternal salvation; and
3. help fellow Christians focus their attention on the final victory of Christ and on the defeat of Satan and his followers.

Note for the small-group leaders: Lesson notes and other materials you will need begin on page 75.

For the Lecture Leader

Session Plan

Worship

Begin the session with the hymn printed in the study leaflet. Accompaniments are available in denominational hymnals, such as *Lutheran Service Book* or *Lutheran Worship* (refer to hymnal index). (Note: Concordia Publishing House has available *The Concordia Organist*. All the initial worship hymns in the LifeLight courses are included in this resource. It's especially helpful for mission congregations and small parishes. See the list of study resources on page 7.)

Prayer

O Victorious Savior and Lord, without Your protection and care, we would be defeated and lost; but Your victory over sin, death, and the devil gives us courage and strength to face every problem and danger in hope and confidence. Keep us in that faith, for Your love and mercy's sake. Amen.

Lecture Presentation

Introduction

Among the most prevalent teachings of the popularizers of the theme of the Last Days in the world today is the expectation of the millennium, a literal thousand-year period in which Christ will rule the world before the final judgment and the end of the world. This view is technically called premillennialism, because its advocates declare that Christ will return before the millennium gets under way and will rule the nations "with a rod of iron" (the New International Version translates this as "with an iron scepter" [Revelation 2:27; 12:5; 19:15]) from Jerusalem.

Premillennialists teach that when Christ returns the believing dead will be raised to rule with Christ on earth and that the world will continue with believers and unbelievers mixed together throughout the millennium. Satan will be bound so that God's people will hold sway in the world, while the ungodly, though continuing to live in the world, will find their power suppressed. The rule of Christ will result in the conversion of the bulk of the Jewish nation, and more people will come to faith during this time. At the end of the millennium Satan will be unleashed for one final battle, in which he and his forces will finally be destroyed. Then the resurrection of the ungodly and of those who died during the millennium will take place, which will be the second resurrection. The ungodly will then be condemned and subjected to the "second death," that is, eternal death.

These beliefs are held in common by both "historic" premillennialists, who often accept the premillennial reign of Christ simply because it seems to be supported by Revelation 20, and by "dispensational" premillennialists, who concoct elaborate schemes concerning the distinction between Israel and the church, who confine the tribulation to seven years before the return of Christ, and who see Revelation as the key to interpreting the rest of Scripture's prophecies rather than vice versa. Christ will return, they say, and will set up an earthly kingdom and rule for a thousand years before He brings the world to an end and establishes the new heavens and the new earth, the church dwelling in heaven and Israel on earth.

Though not common now, there also has existed in some parts of the church a teaching known as postmillennialism, which promises that the teachings of Christ will slowly pervade the whole world so that it will be substantially won for Christ. The present age will thereby gradually fade into a millennium in which Christianity will have so thoroughly permeated the world that evil will be suppressed virtually everywhere, and Christ will return to a world that will be for the most part Christian. This hope is based on their interpretation of Christ's promise that before the end comes the Gospel will have been spread throughout the world. Then, at the end of this time of peace, there will be a short time of apostasy, which will be brought to an end by Christ's return.

Postmillennialism tends to rise during those times and in those places in which the church has wide influence and popularity, and the world has relative peace and prosperity, such as the Western world in the late-nineteenth century and again to a certain extent in the 1950s. It then fades away in times of uncertainty and strife, as it becomes clear once again that the world is in fact by nature at enmity with God and that only a faithful remnant will be saved. In truth, times of upheaval are not minor setbacks on the road to the millennium; they are the normal course of events to be expected in a world that has set itself against God.

There is no question but that a period of "a thousand years" is mentioned in Revelation 20. However, in all of the recorded words of Christ He spoke concerning His return and in all of the other New Testament references to that event (1 Thessalonians 4; 1 Corinthians 15; and 2 Peter 3), there is no mention of a millennial reign of Christ on earth. The return of Christ is always spoken of with finality. The days before His return are referred to as the *last* days (2 Peter 3:3; 2 Timothy 3:1; Acts 2:17). Though the term is not specifically used in Scripture of the day of Christ's return, the church has always recognized that these last days, stretching from Christ's ascension to His return, will culminate in the Last *Day*; the day in which Christ returns as judge. At that time heaven and earth will pass away. There will be no thousand-year period before that happens.

All attempts to squeeze a millennium into the picture arise by reading the reference to a thousand years back *into* the rest of the New Testament rather than interpreting Revelation *by* the rest of the Scriptures, as the earliest readers knew had to be done. In view of the silence of the rest of the Scriptures on the subject, and in view of the fact that the numbers and times of Revelation are to be understood and interpreted symbolically, it is clear that a literal thousand-year reign of Christ on earth cannot be derived from the Scriptures at all and therefore not from Revelation 20. In fact, Christ is quite adamant in declaring that His kingdom is not of this world (John 18:36).

Those who see the necessity of such a kingdom see the need of a time in which Christians can be vindicated in the eyes of the world before the end, a time of visible triumph. They also see the necessity for Christ to rule a physical kingdom before the end comes. Christ's words, and Scripture's continual admonition that God's people will live under the cross until the end comes, eliminate any need for such a kingdom, and in fact show such a belief in such a kingdom to be a misunderstanding of both the Scriptures and of the nature of Christ's reign. This theory seeks glory in this world, where none is to be found.

1 Satan Bound for a Thousand Years (Revelation 20:1–3)

Now that we have seen what Revelation 20 does *not* say, we can get down to the business at hand to see what the text *does* say, for that is where we find the comfort and consolation that these words have to offer. The seventh and final vision begins with an angel coming down from heaven with the key to the bottomless pit—the abyss—to hell itself, and holding a chain. The angel seizes the dragon, who is explicitly identified as Satan, and binds him for a thousand years—that he might not deceive the nations for this period.

Since the number 1,000 signifies completeness, the thousand-year period is to be identified as the complete New Testament era, a specific length of time set and known only by God Himself. During this time Satan himself is not allowed to deceive the nations; that is, the Gospel is allowed free course throughout the world, and Satan can do nothing to prevent it. The chain does not bind him so that he is immobile; rather it keeps him on a short leash. God allows him some movement, some activity, but he cannot prevent whole nations from hearing the message or coming to faith. Only at the end, at the time shortly before Christ's return, will he be released again for a short time and again be allowed to deceive the nations, and if it were possible (which it is not!), even the elect of God. That will be the time of great apostasy spoken of by Paul (2 Timothy 3:1–9) and by Christ Himself (Matthew 24:9–13, 21–25), as Satan seeks one last time to overthrow the kingdom of God.

Note that the prime actor in these events is God. Satan likes to terrify the world with his power, showing himself as a "roaring lion" (1 Peter 5:8) before whom all humanity must stand terrified. While it is true that we are to be wary of Satan as he seeks to deceive and destroy us, these verses show us that the drama directed toward the end is God's drama, and in the end the devil is held in check by God's power. Satan is allowed to go only as far as God allows him to go, and even in that short time immediately preceding the end Satan is set free; he does not escape. God uses and will continue to use Satan to show the consequences of sin, the evil nature of this world's order, and ultimately His judgment against all sin.

2 The First Resurrection (Revelation 20:4–6)

The vision continues as the apostle sees thrones on which were seated "those to whom the authority to judge was committed," that is, all who have overcome, who have remained faithful (Revelation 3:21). Specifically mentioned are the souls of those who have been beheaded because of their testimony of Jesus. In an age of intense persecution, God assures His people through the apostle John that even those who have died for the faith, indeed especially those people, have the hope of reigning with Christ.

Their special traits are mentioned—they refused to worship the beast or to receive the mark of the beast, preferring instead the seal of Christ Himself: the sign of the cross and the seal of Baptism. These are the people who are said to come to life and reign with Christ for the thousand-year period. Since John specifically declares that it is the *souls* of those who were beheaded who live and reign with Christ, the living and reigning take place in heaven and not on earth. As long as Christ reigns from heaven, seated at the right hand of the Father, His saints reign with Him.

This living and reigning is called the "first resurrection." Since it is souls who live and reign, this first resurrection cannot be the return from physical death that will take place on the Last Day. Rather, it is conversion, for it is then that the believer "has passed from death to life" (John 5:24).

On several occasions the Scriptures refer to conversion as a resurrection. In discussing Baptism St. Paul declares that we are to count ourselves dead to sin and alive to God in Christ (Romans 6:11). In Ephesians 2:4–6 he tells us that God has made us, who were dead in transgressions, alive in Christ and has raised us with Christ and seated us with Him in the heavenly realms—a precise description of what John sees in his vision in Revelation 20! Our conversion is truly the first resurrection—and every bit the miracle that the resurrection on the Last Day will be!

John goes on to note that the rest of the dead did not come to life until the thousand years were ended. Those who do not come to know Christ have remained in death. They have not partaken of the first resurrection, remaining separated from God, so that at the resurrection on the Last Day they will be restored only to physical life. Rather than experiencing the real life that God desires for all people, they will be subjected to the "second death," eternal separation from God, condemned and punished by Him forever.

That is why John here records the fifth beatitude of Revelation: "Blessed and holy is the one who shares in the first resurrection!" (v. 6). He explains the reason for this blessedness: those who have partaken of the first resurrection have escaped the power of the second death. Having received the gift of life, they no longer stand under condemnation but instead reign with Christ for a thousand years as His priests, people able to approach the throne of God and stand in righteousness because they have been clothed in the righteousness of Christ. From the moment of faith onward, they live under the continued blessings of God, and not even physical death can remove them from those blessings. They continue in an unbroken stream into eternity.

Since an earthly thousand-year reign of Christ must be rejected, the position set forth here has sometimes been called *amillennialism*, meaning "no millennium." Actually, that is an inappropriate term, for it is not a matter of denying a thousand-year reign of God's people with their Lord but rather a matter of interpreting it properly. A better term than *amillennialism* would be *realized millennialism*, which testifies that the "thousand-year" reign is going on even now as Christ reigns over the universe with His saints. As long as this world lasts, God's people live under the shadow of the cross and perceive the glory that is in store for them only by faith. But by faith we also have the assurance that all who are faithful even to death and through death are in fact even now rulers of the world with Christ in heaven.

3 The Final Battle (Revelation 20:7–10)

At the end of the "thousand years," when Satan is released from his prison, he will again go out to deceive the nations. This will begin the great apostasy, as Satan gathers his forces and attempts one last time to overthrow Christ's rule. The battle mentioned here is the battle of Armageddon. The forces set against God are named Gog and Magog, names taken from Ezekiel 38–39. Magog is mentioned in Genesis 10:2 and in 1 Chronicles 1:5, which are genealogical tables, as a son of Japheth. As with all of the names in these contexts, the man's name becomes the name of the nation he sires. The location of the actual nation of Magog cannot be determined precisely, as the name does not occur again in the Scriptures until mentioned by Ezekiel, and then not again until Revelation 20.

Some people today are preoccupied with the prophecies of Revelation and insist upon their literal fulfillment in our age. They seek to identify some of the place names mentioned in Ezekiel 38–39 with Russia and some of its cities (e.g., "Meshech" with Moscow), in an effort to prove that the battle mentioned here involves Russia's invasion of Israel. But they have no evidence to substantiate their claim. Gog, whose name only occurs in Ezekiel 38–39 and Revelation 20:8, is the prince of Magog. In Revelation these names are symbolic and represent the ungodly powers of this world who are inspired by Satan to oppose and attempt to wipe out God's kingdom, His work in this world.

As the greatest threats to Old Testament Israel were always from the north (preeminently, Assyria and Babylon), so Gog, leading Magog, threatens from the north as well. In fact, the location of Magog to the north makes it the perfect nation to symbolize Satan's final army that seeks to overthrow God's chosen people. As in Ezekiel, so in Revelation, God shows Himself to be completely in control of history. Though the enemies of God surround "the beloved city" (believers, of which the physical city of Jerusalem is a representation), God will not allow it to be destroyed. In 2 Kings 19 the Assyrian army surrounding Jerusalem was put to death as it prepared to attack the city God loves. So now we see God preventing the final attack of the ungodly powers of this world, led by the devil, against God's people by casting fire from heaven.

In chapter 19 the focus was on the destruction of Satan's agents, the beast and the false prophet, that is, the Antichrist and Anti-Spirit, his power and propaganda. Now the focus is on the destruction of Satan himself. Satan is thrown into the lake of fire and sulfur, the same lake used for the destruction of his agents, not to be annihilated, but to be punished forever. They who dared to try to exalt themselves and take the power and majesty that rightfully belong to God alone now will spend eternity under the wrath of that same God.

4 The Judgment (Revelation 20:11–15)

With the destruction of Satan and his agents, God now turns His attention to all who have ever lived on this earth. At the resurrection at the end of time, the One who sits on the "great white throne" has such an imposing and holy presence that even the earth and the sky, which belong to the old order, flee from His presence. The world as we know it is no more. All attention is to be focused on the One who is seated on the throne, that throne which Paul calls "the judgment seat of God" (Romans 14:10) and "the judgment seat of Christ" (2 Corinthians 5:10).

All of the dead, all of those who have ever lived on the earth, from Adam and Eve onward, have been raised to life, for even the sea has given up its dead, as have death and Hades themselves. All now stand before the judgment seat of God—and the books are opened. That stark statement, the "books were opened," is taken from Daniel 7, as Daniel is granted a vision of the Last Judgment and sees the Ancient of Days, God Himself, seated on His throne. The day of reckoning has come. The accounts are laid bare, and each person is judged according to what he or she has done, according to what has been recorded in the books. The accounts of each person's activity are set before the world. Jesus, as He relates the coming of the King for judgment in Matthew 25:31–46, points to how each Christian has treated "My brothers," fellow Christians in need. This basis therefore points to faith—the recognition that in serving the members of His mystical body, the church, we are in fact serving Him. (Christians, of course, are also called to do good to all people but "especially to those who are of the household of faith" [Galatians 6:10].)

Yet, while this judgment seems to take place on the basis of works, there is another, all-important factor involved. Those whose names are written in the Book of Life will ultimately be saved, and those whose names are not there will be cast into the lake of fire, along with death and Hades themselves. But how do we get our names into the Book of Life? The answer, of course, is "We don't." Our names have been written in that book since before the foundation of the world. Having foreknown His people, God has brought them to faith in His Son and kept them in that faith through great tribulation until the end, when He publicly declares them to be not guilty. It is by faith, not by works, that we are saved. Jesus separates the sheep from the goats on the basis of their faith or unbelief. He then points to works as the public, visible evidence of faith (Matthew 25:31–46). God's forgiveness in Christ covers the sins of the believers. It is His forgiveness and His Spirit that empower Christians to do good works—not *in order* to be saved, but because they *are* saved! When those who do not know Christ are judged, they can only be judged as sinners, and so their evil works come forth.

For us who follow Christ, our sins have been cast "into the depths of the sea" (Micah 7:19). Christians need not fear this "final audit," expecting to hear all of our sins presented before the world, for these have all been wiped away by Christ. We, as all people, will be judged by our works, but by God's grace only our good works remain. We will be judged on the basis of our works in order that the world may see that our faith has made a difference in our lives. By means of this last, public judgment, God's people are vindicated in the eyes of the world, and the rest of the world stands condemned, as it deserves to be. But we are still saved by grace. The verdict has already been pronounced, and we live now knowing that we stand *not guilty* before God. We have already passed from death to life. Those who do not believe are condemned already precisely because they have refused to believe in the one whom God has sent (John 3:18).

The judgment, then, upon those who have refused to believe is that which Satan and his agents received—to be thrown into the lake of fire. This is the second death—the death of eternal separation from God, to be utterly abandoned by Him, and to stand under His wrath forever. Hell consists of both abandonment and punishment. God's enemies must be cast from His presence forever, that they may no longer plague the people of God and detract from the joy that God has in store for His people. Having rejected the forgiveness that God offers, they also open themselves to receive the full force of God's wrath, which they so richly deserve.

Even death and Hades are thrown into the lake of fire. Death entered the world because of sin. Hades is that place where those who die apart from Christ are kept and experience the pangs of God's judgment until the time of final judgment. At the resurrection, their purpose is finished. Death has been undone and Hades has been emptied. All vestiges of the consequences of sin in the world have now been done away with. Sin is a part of the old order. The old order, which met its defeat with the death and resurrection of Jesus, now passes away, cast into the lake of fire, and the new order is about to begin.

Conclusion

As the Book of Revelation draws to a close, as does this study of the book, the final hope for the people of God is set forth as the goal for which we now continue to strive. Next week, we conclude the study by setting our sights on that goal.

Concluding Activities

Speak a brief prayer, praising Jesus for this time in which the Gospel is being spread throughout the world. Pray for His blessing upon our own witness to the Gospel. Then make any necessary announcements and distribute study leaflet 9. Remind participants that this LifeLight course will conclude next week and tell them about arrangements for the next LifeLight course.

Our Victorious Lord Reigns Forever

Revelation 21–22

Preparing for the Session

Central Focus

The purpose of God's action on our behalf in history is to bring us back to where He intended us to be in the beginning—in complete fellowship with God in bliss and perfection. We joyfully anticipate the coming of our Lord to bring to completion all He has begun.

Objectives

That participants, led by the Holy Spirit, will

1. appreciate the problems of interpreting apocalyptic writing, but at the same time rejoice in the central message of Christ's certain victory over Satan for all eternity;
2. look joyfully for the return of our Lord and recognize the importance of being prepared at all times for His return; and
3. be encouraged to continue to read and study the Book of Revelation personally and in fellowship with other believers for comfort and encouragement in Christian faith and life.

Note for the small-group leaders: Lesson notes and other materials you will need begin on page 78.

For the Lecture Leader

Session Plan

Worship

Begin the session with the hymn printed in the study leaflet. Accompaniments are available in denominational hymnals, such as *Lutheran Service Book* or *Lutheran Worship* (refer to hymnal index). (Note: Concordia Publishing House has available *The Concordia Organist.* All the initial worship hymns in the LifeLight courses are included in this resource. It's especially helpful for mission congregations and small parishes. See the list of study resources on page 7.)

Prayer

Merciful Father, whose dear Son, our Lord Jesus Christ, rose victorious over death and the grave, we remember with thanksgiving Your faithful people who have trusted in Christ, whose tears are gone and whose sorrows You have turned into joy; and we humbly implore You to strengthen us in the confident hope of the resurrection of the dead and the life of the world to come; through our Lord Jesus Christ. Amen!

Lecture Presentation

Introduction

The struggles of everyday life and the ending of life in death show that something is drastically wrong with the world. Terrorists and fear of terror permeate life, and people long for a "new age," in which hatred will give way to love and peace and happiness.

The human race, some believe, has the power to do all that is necessary to bring this new age about.

We know, however, that no new age will dawn by human effort. All that humanity gets by its own efforts is destruction. Our study of Revelation has shown this to us quite vividly. Yet, God does hold out hope for a new age. Life in the new age, in the new heaven and the new earth, has come to us through the work of Jesus Christ on our behalf. It is a promised reality.

Through seven sets of visions God has shown "the things that must soon take place" (Revelation 1:1). He has shown us that the events of history are in fact scenes of a cosmic battle between the forces of God and the forces of evil, and that Satan and his hosts will in the end be destroyed by God's direct intervention. These things are told us to admonish us to remain faithful, but also to give us comfort in the face of the trials that will come.

Each series of visions has looked at the end times from a slightly different standpoint than the previous ones. With chapter 20 we finally saw the full results of God's judgment—the destruction of Satan, death, Hades (where the unbelieving dead were kept until the final judgment), and all of unrepentant humanity in the lake of fire, which is hell; not destruction in the sense of annihilation, but destruction in that all have been cast from God's presence for eternity and have no more part to play in history. They remain for eternity utterly abandoned by God and under the full brunt of His wrath.

With the wicked now cast from God's presence forever, He turns the vision to the consummation toward which He has been directing history. He describes the "new age" in detail. Again, the numeric imagery and the Old Testament imagery remain as focal points.

1 New Heaven, New Earth, New Jerusalem (Revelation 21:1–8)

Verse 1—John is shown a new heaven and a new earth as the dwelling place of His people, a place "in which righteousness dwells" (2 Peter 3:13). Jesus tells us that heaven and earth will pass away (Matthew 24:35), and so they will. Yet He will prepare the new heaven and earth as an eternal dwelling place for His people.

What is the nature of this new heaven and earth? Does it have any connection at all with the old? Peter's description of the destruction of the old, "The heavens will pass away with a roar, and the heavenly bodies will be burned up and dissolved, and the earth and the works that are done on it will be exposed" (2 Peter 3:10), illustrates the total destruction of the universe as we know it.

Yet, there are hints that the new heaven and new earth have a relationship to the old, one of renewal rather than of annihilation and creation of an entirely new universe. In Romans 8:18–21 Paul describes creation as it is presently constituted as awaiting our revealing as children of God, that is, awaiting Christ's return, because it has been subjected to frustration and is longing to be liberated from its bondage to decay. Though all of creation will die as each of us has died, so also will creation be restored as we will be restored to life. To speak of a new heaven and a new earth is to speak about a *renewed* heaven and earth, no longer subject to decay, and freed from all evil—a true home of righteousness!

In John's vision the new heaven and new earth have no sea. The chaos associated with the sea, the destruction, and the beasts associated with the sea—including the beast of Satan's power (Revelation 13:1–9)—have been destroyed. Where, in the last times, nations were in anguish at the roaring of the sea (Luke 21:25), this basis for terror is no more. The One who while on earth calmed the raging seas has shown His ultimate mastery over it. The chaos has been overcome, all sources of fear have been destroyed, and God's eternal peace is at hand.

Verse 2—To this new heaven and new earth descends the Holy City, the new Jerusalem, to be the dwelling place of God's people. On earth, the city of Jerusalem had great significance, for it was the city from which the kings of the line of David ruled and from which the Savior King had come. Here was the temple, where the glory of God dwelt. But it was not a perfect city. Ruled by apostate kings, inhabited by rebellious people, the city and the temple were destroyed on more than one occasion, and the temple has not existed for over 1,900 years. Yet, where the earthly Jerusalem, for all of its imperfections, was used by God to bring about our salvation, the new Jerusalem will be the perfect dwelling place of God and His people forever.

The city is prepared as a bride, for the church, Christ's people, who will dwell there. Verse 3—As He promised His people so often in the Old Testament and as He has promised us as well, we will be His people and He will be our God. God will be Immanuel, "God with us," in the fullest sense of that name.

The joys of such a relationship are so marvelous and so profound that they cannot be described in any way except by showing that all of the sorrows of this life will have been banished forever. All pain, tears, mourning, and death will have been eliminated, for their source, the sin that divides person from person and people from God, will have been destroyed. All things truly will be made new, as full, joyful lives are lived out to their fullest potential, without sin getting in the way. The joys of a family reunion, in which laughter comes simply from the joy of the relationships of the people, will be magnified infinitely, for the Father of us all, whom we adore, will be at the center of the celebration, and the celebration will never end.

Verse 5—Now a voice speaks from the throne. In words reminiscent of Jesus' words in John 4:14, the voice of the One who is the Alpha and the Omega, the One who made everything in the beginning and has now made everything new (vv. 6–7), tells John who will receive the gift of the new Jerusalem: those who are thirsty and come to the water of life, the gift won for us by Jesus Christ. Those who through the power of this water overcome the world and all of its trials will receive this as an inheritance, for they will be God's sons. (The word *son* is here used as a legal term to refer to official standing that gives the person the right to inherit from the father—in God's usage it has no relationship to gender.)

An inheritance is not something earned. It is given to the heirs as a result of their relationship to their father. So, too, an inheritance comes by a death. In this case it is not the death of a father, but it is the death of the Son, who now empowers us to overcome the world. Those who do not overcome, who instead engage in acts that show contempt for God, will suffer the second death.

Verse 8—It perhaps grates on our ears to hear again of the coming destruction of the wicked amid the beauties of the description of the new age, but God is here speaking through John to us who continue to live in this age to again admonish us to faithfulness and to warn the ungodly that they may repent. Those who continue to rebel against God will have no part in that age. Now is the time to repent!

2 New Jerusalem Close Up (Revelation 21:9–27)

Verse 9—One of God's angels, indeed one who was instrumental in bringing about the final destruction of God's enemies, since he had held one of the bowls of the seven last plagues, now comes to John to show him the new Jerusalem, the bride of the Lamb, in more detail. Since the bride of Christ was purchased by His blood, the focus now turns from the theme of creation, God's making all things new, to redemption.

Verse 11—The imagery here has many allusions to the new temple and city described in Ezekiel 40–48, which are God's ideal, for they were never built on earth. To express the value, the richness of this holy city, the city is described as a precious jewel, though it does not shine with its own radiance, but rather with the glory of God. The perfection of the city is seen in the use of the number 12 (for the Old Testament and New Testament church, the 12 tribes and the 12 apostles) and 1,000 (the cube of 10), signifying absolute completeness. The 12 gates to the city (v. 12) have the names of the 12 tribes, and the 12 foundations of the wall of the city (v. 14) have the names of the 12 apostles, showing that the church has indeed been built upon the foundation of the apostles and prophets (Ephesians 2:20).

Verse 12—At each gate, we are told, stands an angel. At the fall, one of the cherubim was put at the entrance to the Garden of Eden to prevent anyone from entering and gaining access to the tree of life. Now angels stand at the gates of the city not to keep people out, but to welcome the people of God.

Verses 16–17—The perfection of the city is borne out by its measurements, demonstrated by the angel, who measures it out. Twelve thousand stadia in length, breadth, and height, it is a perfect cube of perfect size. The walls are 144 cubits thick (12×12), once again an appropriate number for the church. Verses 18–20—The foundations of the walls are described in terms of precious stones, which again indicate the continuity between the Old Testament and New Testament churches.

The stones mentioned are those that were also placed in the breastplate of the high priest of Israel (Exodus 28:15–21), and each of the stones had engraved in it the name of one of the 12 tribes. Now each of the foundations, each decorated with one of these precious stones, bears the name of one of the apostles. Where stones of such worth were previously worn by only one person, the high priest, now they become foundation stones, supporting the entire priesthood of believers. Verse 21—To complete the picture of priceless value, we are told that each of the gates is made of a single pearl, and the great street of the city is made of gold.

It is no coincidence that the city is described as a cube, the most perfect of shapes. In both the tabernacle and in the temple, the Most Holy Place, the Holy of Holies, was built in the shape of a cube. In this place only the high priest was admitted, and only once a year, on the Day of Atonement. It was in the temple that the ark of the covenant was kept, with the mercy seat that represented God's presence, and so was itself a symbol of heaven.

John tells us that there is no temple in the new Jerusalem, because God and the Lamb are its temple. The Most Holy Place was the place of atonement for the sin of the nation. However, when Christ died, the curtain in the temple that separated the Most Holy Place from the sanctuary was ripped from top to bottom (Matthew 27:50–51). Through His death, the whole human race may now come before the presence of God, and those who put their trust in Christ now do so in the new Jerusalem. All of God's people, the whole church, are now pure and spotless because of Christ. Instead of a temple to signify God's presence among His people, a presence known only by faith, God has now chosen to make His dwelling among His people, so that He Himself now serves as the temple. The New Jerusalem itself is the Most Holy Place because God dwells there with a people whom He has made holy.

Verse 22—Furthermore, just as God showed His glory in the tabernacle and in the temple, so now His glory shines forth in the new Jerusalem. Verse 23—No other lights are needed. The sun and the moon, created to mark the time of the seasons and to divide day and night, are no longer needed, for the light of God's glory shines forever, leading all nations to walk in its light.

Instead of worldwide rebellion, there is worldwide service and worldwide worship. The people of all the nations, all from throughout the world whose names were written in the Book of Life, will come to the city and will be welcomed at all times, for the gates will never be shut. There is no dark to fear, no dangers to be protected from. Nothing impure will enter the city, for nothing impure remains.

3 Life in New Jerusalem (Revelation 22:1–6)

These final visions conclude with the angel showing John the river of the water of life, which flows through the middle of the city. The water of life, promised by Jesus to the Samaritan woman (John 4:14) and again at the Feast of Tabernacles (John 7:37–38), which John identifies with the Holy Spirit (John 7:39), the giver of eternal life, makes this last vision clearly trinitarian, as the river flows from the throne of God and the Lamb. The Lamb accomplishes the work for which the Father sent Him, and the Spirit, the river of life, brings the blessings of that work to each of God's people.

22:2—The final evidence of our complete reconciliation with God is seen in the reappearance of the tree of life, placed in the Garden of Eden in Genesis 2:9 and removed from humanity's grasp because of the fall. What was once forbidden to us because of our sin is now made available to us once again. That relationship that God intended us to have with Him from the beginning is ours once more. Every vestige of the curse of sin has been removed. By His grace, God will take us back to the Garden.

Verse 4—After they had sinned, Adam and Eve hid from God rather than look at Him face-to-face. Indeed, God had declared to Moses that no one could see His face and live (Exodus 33:20). Now, however, it will be possible, indeed it will be our privilege, to look upon the face of God. While those who had received the mark of the beast were banished from His sight and finally destroyed, those who remained faithful received the name of God Himself upon their foreheads, as He had promised (Revelation 3:12).

The angel's final words to John are ones of assurance and encouragement. The words of God are trustworthy and true. God had sent him to show these things that would soon take place because that word can be trusted. God's people may now be prepared for what is to come, for they know their goal.

4 Jesus' Final Words (Revelation 22:7–21)

Verse 7—The book is then brought to a close with words of promise directly from the mouth of Jesus, beginning with the sixth beatitude, "Blessed is the one who keeps the words of the prophecy of this book" (v. 7). The words are kept when we trust that God will bring about what He has promised and when we remain faithful, if necessary even to the point of death.

Verses 8–9—John, overwhelmed with all that he had seen, falls down at the angel's feet to worship him, but the angel, knowing that such honor is due God alone turns John's attention where it belongs, with the admonishment, "Worship God" (v. 9). These words, coupled with the fact that John was not rebuked for falling at the feet of the exalted Lord Jesus in the same manner (Revelation 1:17), show that true worship of God includes worship of Christ as well.

Verse 10—When the prophet Daniel was granted his vision by God, he was told that the revelation he had received was to be shut up and sealed (Daniel 12:4, 9). However, because the time of the end is near—it was then and it is now—John is told *not* to seal up the words of this prophecy. On the contrary, it is to be proclaimed publicly, so that those who have ears may hear. The Word is to be proclaimed as God has set it forth, no more and no less. The curses attached to adding or subtracting from these prophecies are so severe because doing either betrays a lack of trust in the God who is in control in history and a lack of certainty of either His wrath or His grace or both. This Word is to stand on its own, for it is Christ's testimony to the churches.

Verse 14—The seventh and last of the beatitudes calls to mind the host clothed in white of Revelation 7:13–14. They are the ones who are blessed because their robes have been washed in the blood of the Lamb. They have the right—not earned, but graciously given by God—to eat from the tree of life, in the city from which the evil has been excluded. All who desire the righteousness of God, who "hunger and thirst for righteousness" (Matthew 5:6) are invited. The invitation "Come" (Revelation 22:17) is given by the Spirit and the bride, that is, the Spirit issues the invitation through the church. All who hear the message are then commissioned to issue the invitation as well, so that all who are thirsty may receive this free gift, the water of life.

The central focus of these concluding verses, however, is found in Jesus' declaration, "Behold, I am coming soon," a declaration so significant that it is made three times in the last 15 verses of the book. That declaration points first of all to the urgency of getting the message out. As the angel said, "The time is near" (v. 10). Second, it repeatedly assures us that the testimony in this book is true. The trials will come to an end. Satan and his forces will be destroyed. Jesus will return to judge the world and will take His own home to be with Him forever in the new heaven and new earth. That which we long for so fervently is going to come to pass.

Conclusion

Through the visions that God granted to John, we have seen how God has been in control of history and continues to control it, bringing about His own will in the face of the world's rebellion and the stratagems of Satan and his hosts. Though the visions tell of strange, frightening, and wonderful things, the more familiar we become with the entirety of Scripture the more we become able to understand the things that will come to pass as they are recorded here. Those who do not know our Lord find the book to be a closed book, indeed a book written in a code they are not able to solve. We have not only the coded message; we have the key to solving the code as well—the whole of the Scriptures.

With the saints of John's time, indeed with the saints of every age, we look to the consummation of all that is written here in the return of our Lord. Through continued study of this book and the rest of the Scriptures, we keep our hearts set on things above, where Christ is seated at the right hand of God (Colossians 3:1). Having seen what must soon come to pass, and hearing Jesus' assurance, "Behold, I am coming soon," we, too, must respond in exactly the same way John did at the overwhelming joy of this knowledge, and say, "Amen. Come, Lord Jesus!" (v. 20).

Concluding Activities

Make any necessary announcements—especially about the next LifeLight class.

Close on a high note of gratitude and praise, once more utilizing the Common Doxology. Make a few explanatory remarks to make the singing even more meaningful and enthusiastic. Line 1 recognizes *God* as the source of every blessing; line 2 includes all creatures in the praising; line 3 includes also all in heaven; line 4 names each person of the Trinity as the object of our praise. May this be our life now and forever!

Praise God, from whom all blessings flow;
Praise Him, all creatures here below;
Praise Him above, O heaven'ly host;
Praise Father, Son, and Holy Ghost.

Small-Group Leaders Material

Understanding the Book of Revelation

Revelation 1:1–8

Preparing for the Session

Central Focus

To more fully understand this last book of the New Testament and to derive the full comfort and inspiration it can give to dedicated Bible students, it is necessary to recognize the centrality of Jesus Christ as the risen Savior and victorious Lord in the midst of all the problems and persecutions of the early Christians. To gain this understanding, Bible students must be alert to such features of Revelation as apocalyptic writing, frequent Old Testament allusions, and the church-historical approach in interpretation.

Objectives

That participants, led by the Holy Spirit, will

1. gain appreciation of the nature and purpose of apocalyptic writing and its fitting use, considering the historical situation prevailing in the early Christian church;
2. develop a richer understanding and deeper trust in Jesus Christ as the victorious Lord through the varied inspired apocalyptic symbols and pictures; and
3. acquire greater courage and skill to express personal Christian hope more effectively to those enduring trials and tribulations today.

For the Small-Group Leader

The most important aspect of the first meeting of a discussion group is the development of a cordial spirit of genuine concern and appreciation of every member of the group. This is the major responsibility of the leader.

Even in a small group there are different personalities. This fact may cause some embarrassments and even misunderstandings. Let Christian love prevail. John wrote: "Little children, let us not love in word or talk but in deed and in truth" (1 John 3:18).

What blessings the group leader can bring to every session if a genuine spirit of love for all will blossom forth from his or her leadership!

The foremost responsibility of the discussion leaders in the small groups is to promote pertinent discussion of the material that the small-group members have studied during the week. It will, of course, be assumed that the discussion leader has studied the material and arrived at personal answers to the questions in the study leaflets. But the group is served best if the leader guides the group members in discussion before giving a personal answer.

It is also very helpful to use various means to let all members of the group not only to learn the names, but also some biographical facts (e.g. families, occupations, special interests) about each participant to deepen mutual understanding and concern.

Many Christians have never read the Book of Revelation. The apocalyptic form frightens and confuses them. Participants should help one another to a better understanding and consequently a greater appreciation of this precious book of God's comfort.

The golden thread throughout Revelation is the message that Jesus Christ, the Lamb of God and Savior of the world, has proven Himself to be the victorious King of kings and Lord of lords, and that all those who trust in Him will also be victorious over sin, death, and the devil.

Small-Group Discussion Helps

Day 1 • Revelation 1:1–2

1. Immediately and directly this last book of the Bible introduces the message of its contents to us as "the revelation of Jesus Christ." This is the revelation of Jesus Christ, the Son of God, who became man to redeem the world from sin and death. Jesus is both the receiver and the giver of revelation. He passed on the revelation "by sending His angel to His servant John." John's witness is "the Word of God" and "the testimony of Jesus Christ."

2. Apocalyptic features of revelation include references to symbols of angels, animals, and numbers. (a) 4:7–11: four living creatures with six wings and covered with eyes all around; (b) 8:2–6: angels with trumpets and golden censers; (c) 13:18: the number of the beast was 666; (d) 19:17–21: "an angel standing in the sun," a rider on a horse, a beast and a false prophet thrown alive into a lake of fire; (e) 20:2–3: a dragon thrown into a bottomless pit.

3. 2 Timothy 3:16 states explicitly: "*All* Scripture is given by inspiration of God" (KJV). That allows for no excep-

tions. What God has given us by inspiration, including the entire Book of Revelation, must be true because God is Truth. Thus, even though the literary form is different, the content is God's truth for us. Moreover, *all* Scripture, including Revelation, has as its purpose to make the reader "wise for salvation" through faith in Christ, and to equip the Christian for a new life in Christ.

Day 2 • Revelation 1:3

4. (a) Angels were created by God to be His holy messengers. Those who have remained faithful to Him still serve Him in loyalty and devotion. In Revelation 14:6 an angel is seen "flying directly overhead, with an eternal gospel to proclaim to . . . every nation and tribe and language and people." (b) In Revelation 12:9 the leader of the evil angels is identified as "that ancient serpent, who is called the devil and Satan." (c) Hebrews 1:14 tells us that the good angels serve believers, those who will inherit salvation. (d) Only God is to be worshiped. Angels are not God but are creatures and servants of God and, therefore, the angel tells John not to worship him, because "I am a fellow servant with you."

Day 3 • Revelation 1:4–5a

5. The seven churches of Asia Minor that are the addressees are listed in Revelation 1:11: Ephesus, Smyrna, Pergamum, Thyatira, Sardis, Philadelphia, and Laodicea. Locate them on a map. (A map showing the location of these cities is included in the enrichment magazine.)

6. (a) This last book of the Bible is the revelation God the Father gave to Jesus about what the future would hold for the church; Jesus passes along this revelation to the church through John, verse 1. (b) The book is an eyewitness account by John, verse 2. (c) Reader and hearer are blessed, verse 3. (d) Fulfillment is imminent, verse 3. (e) Jesus did all for our salvation, verses 5–6.

7. Other triads in the first five verses: Verse 3: reads . . . hear . . . keep; verse 5: faithful witness . . . firstborn from the dead . . . ruler of kings on earth; verses 5–6: loves us . . . freed us . . . made us a kingdom, priests.

Day 4 • Revelation 1:5b–6

8. (a) Encourage participants to indicate which phrase or phrases they picked and why they picked that phrase. (b) The composite portrait of Christ presented by these terms in Revelation 1:1–8 is verbalized in the theme of the entire Book of Revelation: Jesus Christ is King of kings and Lord of lords forever! Encourage participants to share their word-portraits of Christ.

Day 5 • Revelation 1:7–8

9. **Challenge question.** Encourage participants with this initial attempt at interpreting some of the apocalyptic features of Revelation. (a) 1:4—The seven churches represent the whole church (seven is the number of completeness). (b) 4:4—The 24 elders on the 24 thrones in heaven represent the entire church (perhaps of both Old and New Testaments) ruling with Christ in glory (12 representing the church, reminiscent of the 12 tribes of Israel plus the 12 apostles). (c) 7:4—The 144,000 represents the whole church, all believers, in heaven (12 multiplied by 12 [all believers] multiplied by 1,000 [the entire number, a large number, chosen by God]). (d) 20:3—The thousand years represent the entire period during which Christ will rule His church on this earth through the Gospel (1,000, a large number with definite boundaries set by God). (e) 21: 12, 14, 21—The heavenly city, with its 12 gates guarded by 12 angels, its 12 foundations on which are written the names of the 12 apostles, and the 12 pearls making up the 12 gates represent the church in glory in heaven. Only believers are included; it is founded upon the apostles; it is characterized by glory.

10. (a) Revelation 2:14 (Numbers 24:25) refers to Balaam and Balak, a Midianite king and his hired prophet who attempted to mislead the Israelites; (b) Revelation 2:20 (1 Kings 16:31) refers to Jezebel, a wicked queen who led the Israelites into idolatry; (c) Revelation 5:5 (Genesis 49:8–10) refers to Judah, whose descendant would be the Messiah, the Savior, Jesus; (d) Revelation 7:5–8 (Genesis 49) refers to the tribes of Israel to represent the Old Testament church.

11. The frequent allusions to the Old Testament in the Book of Revelation in consistent agreement and corroboration emphasize the truth of Jesus' statement to the Jews: "Scripture cannot be broken" (John 10:35). They also help us to recognize the continuous importance of Old Testament study as Jesus also stressed to the Jewish woman, "Blessed rather are those who hear the word of God and keep it!" (Luke 11:28 KJV; see Luke 24:25–27).

12. As time permits, let volunteers share. There are many significant truths with which any Christian can identify because Jesus Christ is presented as Savior and Lord forthrightly and forcefully. Perhaps a favorite personal passage will be "To Him who loves us and has freed us from our sins by His blood and has made us a kingdom, priests to His God and Father, to Him be glory and dominion forever and ever. Amen" (Revelation 1:5–6).

The Triumphant Christ Speaks to His Church

Revelation 1:9–3:22

Preparing for the Session

Central Thought

It is a source of joy and comfort to know that Christ gives His message of hope to the church through the ages. Since we live in a sinful world, the church continually struggles with problems from the inside and outside. This week we hear Christ, who has triumphed over all the problems that will ever confront us, even death itself, speaking words of judgment and encouragement to His people and calling them to continued faithfulness.

Objectives

That participants, led by the Holy Spirit, will

1. see that Christ's glorious attributes match the specific needs of each congregation;
2. rejoice in Christ's presence in the midst of His people; and
3. examine their life and the life of their congregation in the light of Christ's standards of judgment as expressed in these letters.

For the Small-Group Leader

This can develop into one of the most productive small-group sessions, as the leader guides the discussion toward a loving, constructive criticism of Christian congregations today in the light of the positive and negative aspects of the seven churches analyzed by Christ Himself in these seven letters.

Small-Group Discussion Helps

Day 1 • Revelation 1:9–20

1. (a) Some questions continue to be asked about the identity of John the author of Revelation. The preponderant opinion of scholars, however, identifies him as John, the son of Zebedee. In these verses John writes about himself as a brother of his readers, one who shares their suffering. In fact, at the time of writing he was under arrest on the island of Patmos. (b) John implies that his readers also are suffering for the sake of Christ. He refers to himself as "your brother and partner in the tribulation and the kingdom and the patient endurance that are in Jesus."

2. (a) On Sunday (the Lord's Day) John was in a state of ecstasy. He heard a loud voice telling him to write a special message to seven churches located in Asia Minor. As John turned in the direction of the voice, he saw seven golden lampstands symbolic of the seven churches mentioned earlier. Among the lampstands John saw the glorious Jesus. In John's vision Jesus is described in terms suggesting wisdom and dignity. Daniel saw a similar vision ("one like a son of man"). Both visions tell us that Jesus is God. In both visions Christ receives power over all, even over death and hell. (b) As John was overwhelmed in the presence of Jesus' majesty, and "fell at His feet as though dead" (v. 17), so we must say that this demonstration of sovereign majesty makes a powerful impression on us. Encourage participants to share their own responses.

3. (a) No matter how holy or powerful or majestic Jesus may show Himself to be, His saving grace shines through. We find the Gospel of Jesus our Savior in the statements: "Fear not, I am the first and the last, and the living one. I died and behold I am alive forevermore, and I have the keys of Death and Hades." Through His death and resurrection, Christ has conquered death and hell for us! (b) Jesus forcefully shows the church that He is most vitally concerned about our eternal security and welfare and that He has all the necessary power and strength to guarantee us that no power will be able to prevent us from being saved. Encourage participants to share their own statements.

4. Jesus stands among the lampstands (churches) and holds their stars (angels, messengers) in His right hand. The right hand represents His power. Jesus promises to be together with those who are gathered in His name, though they be but two or three.

Day 2 • Revelation 2

5. The four churches in the second chapter can be identified as follows: (a) Tempted to compromise: Pergamum; (b) encouraged to be faithful: Smyrna; (c) left its first love: Ephesus; (d) a temptress in its midst: Thyatira.

6. (a) Jesus commends the church in Ephesus for many reasons: its deeds, hard work, perseverance, refusal to tolerate wicked men and false apostles, perseverance and endurance of hardships, and hatred of the practices of the Nicolaitans—a group who wanted Christians to compromise with paganism when it came to public festival, social, and civic activities. (b) Yet He faults the church because it had left its first love; perhaps it no longer embraced the Gospel with its former fervor.

7. (a) Both churches were tolerating idolatry and sexual immorality within their midst. In ancient times these two sins often went together since many pagan religions incorporated sexual immorality in their idolatries. (b) Idolatry (worshiping or trusting in something more than God) continues to be a sin in our own day, although present-day idols may be such things as prestige, power, and personal comfort. Sexual immorality never seems to lose its appeal to the sinful human nature.

Day 3 • Revelation 2

8. Opinions may vary among Christian Bible students as to which church was strongest or weakest, depending upon the emphasis placed upon certain characteristics. As in churches today, weaknesses and strengths differ. Smyrna demonstrated strength by its faithfulness even in persecution. Pergamum showed signs of serious weakness in tolerating false doctrine and practice.

9. Faithfulness is expected of Christians under all circumstances. It takes on special challenge, however, when persecution descends upon us because of our Christian faith and life. Such were the conditions at Smyrna at this time. For that reason Jesus' encouragement to being "faithful unto death" was especially meaningful. The same applies today.

10. The sword coming from Jesus' mouth symbolizes His Word. The two edges may correspond to the Word's two messages: Law and Gospel. Hebrews 4:12 refers to God's Word as a living, active instrument that judges inner thoughts and attitudes.

11. (a) As time permits, let volunteers share their responses. Jesus sees every part of us and of our lives. While the awareness that nothing can be hidden from Jesus may cause us to feel uncomfortable at first, we are reassured by His all-covering grace. Even our secret sins may be forgiven. Jesus' penetrating sight also sees the evidences of our faith, and He sees our troubles and the hardships we bear. All in all, the thought of Jesus' penetrating sight is a thought that comforts us. (b) Let volunteers share their responses. The imagery of burnished bronze feet comfort and encourage us since it assures us that Jesus overcomes the devil and all of those powers allied with him.

Day 4 • Revelation 3

12. Sardis was a very wealthy city ever since the days of Croesus. It was known as a degenerate, pleasure-loving city. Amidst the surroundings of wealth and pleasure, the church there was known as the church that was dying. This church was to wake up and repent and to strengthen what they had left.

13. Jesus is obviously delighted with conditions in the church in Philadelphia, as He shows in His letter. He assures His people in Philadelphia—and also us today—that He holds the key to heaven and has opened heaven to us. Because Jesus holds that key, no one can shut heaven's door against us. We also have opportunities to show the open door to heaven to others as we point them to Jesus as their Savior from sin.

14. (a) The church in Laodicea became known as "the lukewarm church." It was, no doubt, influenced by the fact that the city held a prominent position in Asia Minor in banking, in clothing manufacturing, and in medicine. In His letter Jesus chides the church for its materialistic pride in saying, "I am rich, I have prospered, and I need nothing" (3:17). He urges repentance and promises to come to them and bless them. (b) How fitting today! Jesus also addresses us in our comfortable, materialistic setting; He urges us to repent of our materialism and to receive His grace. Encourage participants to share their insights.

Day 5 • Review of Revelation 1:19–3:22

15. In the apocalyptic writing of the Book of Revelation, the number 7 is the number of completeness. So we may assume that the seven letters of Revelation 2 and 3, written to the seven churches of Asia Minor, are representative of Christ's communication to all the Chris-

tian churches on earth. Note the repeated statement: "What the Spirit says to the churches" (2:7, 11, 17, 29; 3:6,13, 22). (a) Jesus commends the church in Ephesus for its hard work, perseverance, and resistance to false teachers. He rebukes it because it has forsaken its first love. (b) He commends the church in Smyrna because it has remained faithful despite afflictions and poverty. Though they would soon face persecution, Jesus promises them the crown of life if they continue steadfast. There is no rebuke. (c) Jesus commends the church in Pergamum for remaining faithful despite severe persecution by Satan's agents. He rebukes this church for tolerating some who were willing to compromise their faith. (d) Jesus commends the church in Thyatira for its good deeds. But He rebukes the church because there were false teachers among them. (e) Jesus commends the minority in this church who remained faithful to Him, but He rebukes the majority who have fallen into spiritual deadness. (f) Jesus commends the church in Philadelphia since the Christians there have held on to their faith in Him despite their lack of strength. He encourages them to remain faithful. There is no rebuke. (g) Jesus rebukes the church in Laodicea since it is lukewarm in faith, though it thinks itself well off. He pleads with them to admit Him once more into their midst. There is no commendation.

16. Clearly we may find strengths and weaknesses of the church today in these lists. Encourage participants to share and talk about their responses.

17. **Challenge question.** (a) Answer given. (b) To the church in Smyrna Jesus identifies Himself as the First and the Last (the eternal God) and as the one who died and came to life again (the resurrected Lord). With these characteristics He comforts them in their suffering and promises them life in His eternal kingdom. (c) To the church in Pergamum Jesus identifies Himself as the one who has the double-edged sword (His Word). His Word has and will fight for them as they struggle against persecution and idolatry. (d) To the church in Thyatira Jesus identifies Himself as the Son of God, with blazing eyes and feet of burnished bronze. He sees both their faithfulness and their tolerance of a false teacher who leads them into idolatry and immorality. The Lord will crush her and those who join with her. (e) To the church in Sardis Jesus identifies Himself as the one who holds the seven spirits of God and the seven stars (the pastors). If they do not wake up and repent, they will face the coming Judge. Those who have remained faithful will join the Lord in glory. (f) To the church in Philadelphia Jesus identifies Himself as the one who holds the key of David, the Gospel. With this Gospel they will reach out to others, resist persecution, and endure until their Lord comes to take them into His glorious heaven. (g) To the church in Laodicea Jesus identifies Himself as the Amen, the faithful and true witness, the ruler of God's creation. He, the divine Son of God, can be the only source of the true riches.

18. As time permits, let participants share insights. The triumphant Christ is personally interested in every Christian church on earth; Christ diagnoses every church as to strengths and weaknesses; He applies Law and Gospel appropriately in all His messages to the churches; His one continuing message to all Christian churches is: "I am coming soon. Hold fast what you have, so that no one may seize your crown" (3:11). Every Christian may gain different vivid insights from the seven letters Christ wrote in these first chapters of the Book of Revelation. All may be helpful. When, however, the condition is added: "in the relation of the triumphant Christ to the Christian church today," the focus is narrowed. The theme of the entire book is: "Jesus Christ is King of kings and Lord of lords forever!" What greater insights in regard to that has the participant gained over against world conditions today or the mission of the church at this time or guidance and inspiration for personal Christian life?

Our Victorious Lord Leads through Trouble to Triumph

Revelation 4–7

Preparing for the Session

Central Focus

In the serene picture of God's majesty in heaven we see the victorious Lamb taking the scroll and opening the seals to review the future. Here God shows us the destiny of all people: destruction for the wicked and eternal bliss and joy for those who have "washed their robes . . . in the blood of the Lamb."

Objectives

That participants, led by the Holy Spirit, will

1. learn that all history is in God's hands;
2. get a taste of the eternal peace of heaven; and
3. be urged to set their eyes "on things that are above" (Colossians 3:2).

For the Small-Group Leader

The Small-Group Discussion Leader is the primary leader and key person in the LifeLight program. Why? In many churches only a few people have had training or experience in the unique feature of small-group work, namely, to see to it that every participant really participates without embarrassment but with genuine satisfaction. Since the Book of Revelation is somewhat different in its literary type, some participants will need special encouragement in the early sessions.

Small-Group Discussion Helps

Day 1 • Revelation 4

1. (a) God reigns from heaven over all of creation. He is the heavenly King. (b) God's appearance of a brilliant, unapproachable light emphasizes His majesty and holiness. (c) The rainbow is reminiscent of the covenant God made with the earth following the flood. God is the God who graciously covenants with people. (d) Christians will rule in heaven with the Lord. We will share in His glory. This wonderful privilege will come about not because Christians have deserved it but because God graciously promises it. (e) Christ has purified His church with His own blood. In heaven Christians will be pure and holy, just as God sees us now as pure and holy for the sake of Christ, our Savior. The Sea may represent holiness—the holiness of God Himself and the holiness God gives His people through Jesus. (f) God is the Lord of all creation, which praises and glorifies Him.

2. (a) The lesson God wants to teach John and all of God's people through the revelation given to John is that He is in complete control of all things. He is the almighty King and Lord of heaven and earth. Therefore, when we are afraid, we can trust in Him for courage. (b) This fact is also encouraging to us as individual Christians. God, our King and Savior, is stronger than anything that threatens us and is well able to save us from anything.

3. The holiness and almighty, creative power of God is the theme of these songs sung by creation and the saints in heaven. These songs acknowledge God as Lord and King.

Day 2 • Revelation 5

4. (a) God's right hand symbolizes His power and strength. He is able to overcome all opponents. That the scroll is held in God's right hand indicates that He has control of the future. (b) "Lion of the tribe of Judah" refers to Christ, the descendant of Judah who was named "a lion's cub" and promised the right to rule until He comes to "Him who was seated on the throne" (v. 7). "Root of David" is also a messianic reference. All but destroyed by the Assyrians, the "stump" of Jesse (David's father) yet sends up a new shoot from its roots, the Savior in whom also the Gentiles will hope. The rich Old Testament imagery would assure John that Christ alone was worthy—and could—open the scroll.

5. (a) This reference to Christ has rich meaning, rooted in Old Testament events and prophecy. The unblemished lamb sacrificed at Passover pointed forward to Jesus, the sinless Lamb of God who would be sacrificed

to pay the penalty of the sin not only of God's Old Testament people, Israel, but of *all* people—the Gentiles. (b) Encourage participants to share the paragraphs they wrote, expressing their praise to Jesus. Rejoice together in the praises that are expressed.

Day 3 • Revelation 6

6. As the Lamb opens each of the seven seals, events that are to take place on the earth are revealed by symbolic images that appear. The same events revealed through this vision are described by Jesus in Matthew 24:5–14; Mark 13:6–13; and Luke 21:8–17. The first four symbolic images in this vision given to John are four horsemen riding horses of different colors. (a) The white horse and its rider represent the deceptions of false Christs and those who claim to speak in His name but do not. Such deceptive, false teachers mislead many to their ruin. The white color of the horse represents victory and the righteousness of God's kingdom, but in this case it is falsely worn and represents the deceptiveness of these anti-Christian teachers. (b) The red horse and its rider represent the warfare among nations that will characterize much of world history until Christ's return. The sword carried by this horseman is large since many people will be killed by war. The red color of the horse represents bloodshed. (c) The black horse and its rider represent famine and the many other disasters people will suffer throughout the remaining history of this world. The scales and the high prices charged for food indicates the scarcity in times of famine and disaster. (d) The pale horse and its rider represent death and Hades (hell), which will swallow people up, many through the war and disasters represented by the previous two horses and riders.

7. The opening of the fifth seal reveals the persecution Christians will suffer in this age before Christ returns. Martyrs (Christians whose testimony results in suffering and death for Christ's sake) are represented by the souls under the heavenly altar. They are clothed with white robes (white, the color of victory and righteousness) since they are covered with the righteousness of Christ, their Savior, and they are asked to be patient until this age shall have been completed, and they will be vindicated.

8. The opening of the sixth seal represents the return of Christ at the end of this age to bring the judgment of God upon the earth. This will be a great calamity to all unbelievers and especially to all who persecuted the church and opposed the Gospel. The return of Christ to the earth is introduced by the signs that occur in the sky.

9. In this period before Christ returns, believers may expect that the events revealed by the opening of the first six seals will occur, even while most ignore them until Christ suddenly returns. Christians are to remain faithful and expectant throughout this period, ready and prepared for the Lord's coming, so that they are not caught unaware but are found faithful and believing when the Lord returns.

Day 4 • Revelation 7:1–8

10. Before the judgment of the world takes place at the return of Christ, believers are sealed—marked so as to be spared from condemnation in the judgment. (a) The Israelites were sealed (marked for preservation) when the destroying angel passed through Egypt by the blood of the Passover lambs that was painted on the doors of their houses. The destroying angel passed over such houses and did no harm to the inhabitants of those houses. (b) Abraham and his descendants were sealed with circumcision to mark them as those whose faith in the coming Savior preserved them as righteous before God. (c) God has sealed Christians with the Holy Spirit, whose presence within us is a guarantee that we will inherit eternal life in God's glorious kingdom.

11. (a) The 144,000 who are sealed represent not only faithful Israelites but also New Testament believers—the entire church throughout the ages. The combination of 12, the number representing the church, and 10, the number representing completeness—both numbers multiplied—is an assurance that *all* believers will be saved. (b) What a wonderful comfort this is to us—a comfort given by the assurance of Jesus, our Good Shepherd, that we will not perish but have everlasting life in His kingdom, and that no one can snatch us away from Him!

Day 5 • Revelation 7:9–17

12. Who will be in heaven with Christ and the holy angels for all eternity? "A great multitude that no one could number, from every nation, from all tribes and peoples and languages." (Four groups are mentioned; four is the number that represents the earth.)

13. The white robes worn by the saints in heaven represent the righteousness given to them by their Savior,

the Lamb who died for them to make them holy. The palm branches in their hands represent the victory that is theirs through their victorious Savior, Jesus Christ.

14. The saints in heaven give all credit and honor to God and to the Lamb for their being in heaven. They claim no credit for themselves. Their salvation has been by grace alone, through Christ.

15. Encourage participants to share the phrases that mean the most to them personally. Certainly there is much in this wonderful description to comfort and encourage all participants as they think of their own future life in God's glorious, eternal kingdom and as they think about those who have preceded them into that kingdom through death.

16. As time permits, encourage participants to share their lists. Blessings inspiring confident hope and victorious gratitude are ours now already, even though we are still in the church on this earth, undergoing suffering and various trials. God is in control no matter what trials the church may encounter. God's promises are guaranteed by His love. Final victory will come suddenly but surely. The songs of praise sung by God's people on earth and in heaven declare God's sovereignty and majesty; rainbows reveal His mercy and grace. God reveals Himself as He wills by His Word. Redemption comes through faith in Jesus Christ. All the honor enjoyed by God's redeemed saints is derived from Him whom they serve.

The World Shaken, God's Kingdom Stands Firm

Revelation 8–11

Preparing for the Session

Central Focus

We know that God is firmly in control of history. When we look at the world around us, however, it sometimes seems as though this is not the case. In our Bible study this week, we see that even though the world seems to be falling apart around us, God's kingdom stands firm and secure.

Objectives

That participants, led by the Holy Spirit, will

1. continue to be aware of signs of disturbance and destruction being present in every age of world history;
2. be convinced that "the kingdom of the world has become the kingdom of our Lord"; and
3. be grateful for the constant evidence of the triumph of the kingdom of God.

For the Small-Group Leader

This is the fourth session of the small group. By this time certain characteristics of individuals have begun to show themselves, and it is helpful if the small-group leader can skillfully mold them into a unit of Bible students that truly appreciate each other's gifts. Give hearty approval to answers that demonstrate true biblical understanding, and be gentle and kind and yet firm in correcting errors. Constantly emphasize the one great purpose of being built up together in the Lord.

Small-Group Discussion Helps

Day 1 • Revelation 8

1. The smoke of the incense as it rises to God is accompanied by the prayers of the saints (believers). That this symbolism of the smoke of the incense was commonly understood we see from Psalm 141:2. As the priest in the temple burned incense on the altar of incense, people outside prayed (Luke 1:10).

2. **Challenge question.** The hurling of the censer of burning incense to the earth represents the fact that God had answered the prayers of His suffering people and was going down to deliver them by bringing judgment upon their persecutors.

3. While not all of the plagues visited upon Egypt are represented in this vision—and those represented are not in the same order—several of the plagues are suggested in this vision, and other aspects of the Exodus from Egypt are suggested as well. (a) The first trumpet brings hail mixed with fire and blood. This suggests the seventh plague upon Egypt, a plague of deadly hail. (b) The second trumpet turns water into blood. This suggests the first Egyptian plague, when water was turned to blood. (c) The fourth trumpet produces darkness. This suggests the ninth plague upon Egypt, when that land was plunged into darkness. (d) The similarities lead us to see this vision as telling us of the rescue of God's people and of God's judgment upon those who oppose the Lord.

4. The third trumpet turns water bitter and poisonous. This judgment of God is the opposite of what occurred at Marah during the Israelites' journey in the desert, when God turned bitter, undrinkable water sweet. God, in His grace, is able to sweeten the bitter experiences of life, but He is also able to bring judgment upon sinners by those same experiences.

5. Jesus predicted that signs including natural disasters would occur in the world to indicate that He would soon return to this earth with power and glory to judge all mankind.

Day 2 • Revelation 9:1–21

6. The bottomless pit, or abyss, or hell, is the place where the devil and his evil angels (demons) and those people who are in the devil's kingdom are confined "in prison" (1 Peter 3:19) for all eternity. It is a place of indescribable torment. Burning fire indicates pain; darkness, the horror of separation from God.

7. (a) Peter warns us that the devil desires to devour us—to eat us up! If we yield and give in to him, he will

certainly destroy our hope for heaven. Nevertheless, the devil remains on a chain held by God and he cannot do anything that is not allowed by God. (b) *For personal reflection. Sharing optional.* Move on to the next question unless someone wants to comment on this "exercise" intended for private devotion.

8. The horde released by the fifth trumpet might torture and sting, but they could not kill (though those whom they afflicted might long for death). The army released by the sixth trumpet, however, killed a third of mankind. This shows that their power and devastation is much greater than the horde released by the fifth trumpet.

9. God is able to use even the powers of evil to accomplish His gracious purpose. The Lord's intent is that people might repent under the powerful onslaught of the army of demons from hell. But so strong and stubborn is the hold of sin that even the horrors brought about by the army from hell is not enough to cause these stubborn sinners to give in and repent.

Day 3 • Revelation 10

10. (a) The rainbow was made a sign of the covenant God made with all creatures after Noah, his family, and his cargo of creatures left the ark, pledging that He would never again cut off all life on the earth with a flood. (b) God guided the Israelites, the people with whom He had made a covenant, through the desert to the Promised Land with a pillar of cloud by day and a pillar of fire by night. (c) When Jesus appeared in His heavenly glory on the mountaintop to Peter, James, and John, His face "shone like the sun." God has made His covenant of salvation with believers through Jesus. The angel's appearance thus tells us that the Judge of all the earth remembers the covenants He has made with all humans and especially with the Israelites. His face identifies Jesus as our Judge, through whom God has made His covenant of grace with us.

11. Peter tells us that what seems like a delay to us in regard to Jesus' coming again in glory to judge humankind shows that God does not regard the sweep of time as we do and that He is giving opportunity for sinners to come to repentance and faith.

12. Note that the scroll that John eats is not the same as the scroll described in Revelation 5. That scroll, which only the Lamb might open, revealed and brought about the events that would happen until the end of time. This little scroll is already open and is to be eaten. This scroll is the proclamation of Law and Gospel that is to be made by the Lord's messengers. Eating it signifies that John is to prophesy, to reveal God's Word concerning "many peoples and nations and languages and kings."

13. (a) Encourage participants to speak about what makes God's Word sweet to them. They may well speak of how God reveals the Gospel of forgiveness, grace, love, and peace to us through Jesus, our Savior, or about the wonderful promises and assurances God gives us in His Word. (b) *For personal reflection. Sharing optional.* After the initial taste of sweetness, the little scroll turned John's stomach sour. Ezekiel also found it a bitter experience to proclaim God's Word to a people who rejected it. Ezekiel was persistently to speak God's Word of judgment upon a stubborn, rebellious people. Speaking God's Word of Law and judgment is never easy. But as parents, co-workers, and friends, we need to speak it in love to recall people to repentance, lest they be eternally lost in their sin. Gently encourage any participant who, by sharing a burden of need to admonish, may be strengthened by the group's loving empathy and prayers.

Day 4 • Revelation 11:1–14

14. The Old Testament temple had an outer court where nonbelievers, or Gentiles, were permitted. "Nations" in Revelation 11:2 represent nonbelievers, those who are not God's people (as Gentiles in the Old Testament were not Jews), even though they claim to be God's people. In the letter to the church in Smyrna Jesus had referred to those Jews who had persecuted Christians as "those who say that they are Jews and are not" and as "a synagogue of Satan." This is certainly no disparagement of them because they were Jews but because they, though they were Jews, rejected and persecuted God's Word. In so doing they put themselves in the category of those Jews whom Jesus called children of the devil (John 8:44). God has limited (or shortened) the time during which Satan may oppose God, persecute His church, and tempt people. Satan knows this and is working all the harder during the time he has left. (a) A similar vision is given to the prophet Zechariah, a prophet who proclaimed God's Word in the time when the Jews returned to the Holy Land after 70 years in exile in Babylon. To Zechariah God revealed that He had raised up two witnesses (revealed to be Zerubbabel the civil ruler and Joshua the high priest). These would serve God by the power of His Spirit, not by human might. So also the two witnesses in John's

vision are empowered by the Holy Spirit. (b) The two witnesses wear sackcloth, a rough cloth similar in this respect to the garment of camel's hair worn by John the Baptist. The witnesses, like John, preach a message of repentance to prepare Jews for the coming of Jesus, the Messiah. John preached to prepare them for Jesus' first coming as the promised Savior; the witnesses for His coming to be judge of all. (c) As Elijah called down fire from heaven, so the two witnesses speak powerfully since they speak God's Law, which finally brings down His wrath on unrepentant sinners.

15. As time permits, let volunteers share their responses.

Day 5 • Revelation 11:15–19

16. Jesus will be seen in the clouds with power and glory. Angels will sound a loud trumpet call, and believers (the elect) will be gathered together from all the earth.

17. The 24 elders give thanks that the time when God will judge all humankind has come, for at that time He will declare believers to be righteous for Jesus' sake and will vindicate His suffering church and punish those who persecuted Christians.

18. Psalm 2 is a prophecy of the triumphal victory of Jesus Christ over all the evil powers of the earth. Through His victory all kingdoms and rulers have been subdued. The reign of God and His Anointed has been established. Jesus Christ is now and will forever be King of kings and Lord of lords. Encourage participants to share their personal statements of trust based on the coming of Christ and His eternal reign.

19. The opening of the temple so that the ark of the covenant can be seen by all signifies that full and free access to God has been given to all those who will live in God's kingdom of heaven due to the atoning work of Jesus.

Christ's Victory over Satan and His Hosts

Revelation 12–14

Preparing for the Session

Central Focus

God is in charge, but Satan persists in trying to defeat Him. This week we see that Satan is vigorously and persistently at work seeking to overthrow God's kingdom and to deceive His people. But we also see that God preserves His people from the strongest assaults of the evil one and his servants and keeps them safe.

Objectives

That participants, led by the Holy Spirit, will

1. see how Satan seeks to overthrow Christ;
2. become more confident of Christ's power to overcome Satan and his hosts; and
3. point others to the victory that Christ has already won over Satan and his hosts.

For the Small-Group Leader

The Romans had a saying: *Repetitio est mater studiorum,* which in translation says to us: "Repetition is the mother of studies." This is an important principle to remember for getting the most out of these Bible studies. We are now at the center of the nine units. It is time for review and repetition. In the first four cycles we have become acquainted with some of the unique features of apocalyptic writing, used especially in time of trouble. We have heard Christ comfort representative Christian churches in the midst of persecution and have also been assured of His certain triumph, no matter how the world may be shaken with storms and plagues.

Time is limited for discussion and review, but if the small-group leader is well prepared, repetition will serve to save time and increase retention. Whatever you do, keep the overall schedule intact.

Small-Group Discussion Helps

Day 1 • Revelation 12

1. (a) **Challenge question.** The woman about to give birth represents the faithful people of God, the church. From God's faithful people of the Old Testament, the children of Israel, God brought forth the Savior of the world, the Messiah, Jesus Christ. (b) The child is Jesus Christ, the King of heaven and earth, who came down to this earth to redeem us. (c) The enormous red dragon is identified as Satan, commonly called the devil.

2. (a) The woman's Son is taken back into heaven after He completed His redeeming work. In heaven He rules His church and creation and prepares a place for us in His heavenly kingdom. (b) **Challenge question.** The woman (the church) remains on the earth until Christ returns in glory. Though the church is away from its home in heaven, the church is protected and preserved by God.

3. Jude 9 identifies Michael as an archangel, a chief or ruling angel. He is the only angel identified in the Bible as an archangel. Only one other angel is identified in Scripture by name—Gabriel, who appeared to Zechariah, the father of John the Baptist, and to Mary, the mother of Jesus (Luke 1:19, 26).

4. (a) The good news is that Satan was defeated and thrown out of heaven; the bad news is that he was thrown down to earth, where he continues his warfare against God by attacking God's people. His time on earth is limited to a short period; therefore, he goes about his attack all the more furiously. (b) **Challenge question.** Satan, a chief angel of God, in pride esteems himself greater than God and rebels against Him. Rebelling with him are other angels, who become the evil angels or demons (devils).

5. (a) Though Satan attacks the church, and enlists the aid of his allies in doing so, he will not be able to overcome God's church. In the end, Satan will be completely defeated, and God's people will share in His triumph. (b) We are assured personally that God intends to bring us into His kingdom, that we can depend on Him to do this, and that He will strengthen us and protect us from the devil.

Day 2 • Revelation 13:1–10

6. The beast represents ungodly forces in this world that oppose God and His church on earth. The vision of the beast in Revelation 13:1–2 combines characteristics of the world empires in Daniel's vision (Daniel 7:2–7, 15–22). These powers often take the form of world rulers and governments that oppose the church and the Gospel. In John's day Roman emperors and their officials often persecuted the church, especially when Christians refused to worship the emperor as a god. In the centuries since John's day, many rulers and governments (most recently Communist governments in Eastern Europe and Asia and dictators in the Middle East) have persecuted Christians and opposed the church, as have governments and dictators in other parts of the world.

7. As time permits, share examples and insights. Various Roman emperors allowed themselves to be worshiped as gods (and then began to insist on this worship). Anti-Christian media stars bask in adulation even as they espouse causes and values that are opposed to Christian faith and values.

8. Those who would not worship the beast were either exiled (held as a prisoner at some place away from their homes, as was John himself [Revelation 1:9]) or they were executed (as were the rest of the apostles—James, Paul, and Peter and many others). Though threatened with exile or death, Christians are encouraged to endure patiently and to remain faithful to God, trusting themselves to His care.

9. Paul's own attitude as he faced almost certain execution for the sake of Jesus is encouraging to us as we attempt to remain faithful to the Lord in our own circumstances. Paul was ready to be sacrificed for the Lord who was sacrificed for him. He looked back at his life in the Lord's service with satisfaction, and he looked forward to being welcomed into heaven, where sin would be behind him forever and he would live in righteousness.

Day 3 • Revelation 13:11–18

10. The second beast has some characteristics of a lamb and so resembles the Lamb of God. Jesus warns us about false prophets who wear sheep's clothing (appear nonthreatening and resemble Christians or even the Lamb of God Himself) but are actually ferocious wolves (extremely dangerous to our spiritual life). Included in the examples participants may give are supposedly Christian friends who tempt us to sin because "it isn't really that bad" or "it's okay to do it just this once." They may also mention such things as materialism, sexual "freedoms," and new age.

11. Like the second beast, the first beast also fakes a resemblance to Jesus. The first beast also takes on a characteristic of Jesus with the fatal wound that had been healed, resembling Jesus in His death and resurrection (Revelation 13:3, 12, 14). As Jesus warns in Matthew 24:24, false prophets often identify themselves with Him and perform miraculous signs and wonders as if with His authority and power, but He has not authorized or empowered them.

12. The second beast performs great and miraculous signs in order to deceive people, even Christians, if possible. He wants to trick them into worshiping the first beast. Many Christians in John's day were surrounded by idolatrous religions and were told that they must also worship the Roman emperor as a god. Today Christians hear the voices of cult leaders, some even claiming to be Christ Himself (e.g., the Waco, Texas, cult leader of spring 1993). Insofar as government officials and technology gurus promise utopias here on earth in return for our primary allegiance, they too become fulfillments of this text.

13. Participants may list any number of dictators in our world today.

14. There are two kinds of wisdom—worldly wisdom, which is really a false wisdom since it makes the human mind the measure and judge of all things and calls faith in God a superstition, and godly wisdom, which recognizes the Lord as the source of all that exists. Godly wisdom recognizes unbelief for what it is—rebellion against God—and recognizes those who oppose God for who they are—agents of Satan. Godly wisdom can only come from the Spirit, who gives this godly wisdom to believers in Christ. Note that the Spirit gives wisdom as people feed on the Word about Christ and His redeeming love, meditate on it, and remember and apply it as they day-by-day face choices in their lives. What a strong encouragement to let the Spirit strengthen us through a strong and daily devotional life and through the sharing of the Word as we're doing in LifeLight!

Day 4 • Revelation 14:1–13

15. The Mount Zion mentioned here refers to the heavenly Jerusalem, the temple where God's throne is locat-

ed. The Mount Zion on earth is the site in Jerusalem where the Jewish temple was located.

16. *For personal reflection. Sharing optional.* If time permits, let any volunteers comment. Otherwise move ahead to the next question.

17. The theme of the songs sung by the saints and angels in heaven is praise for Jesus, who redeemed all people by giving His life on the cross. He has made believers kings and priests in God's kingdom. All praise, honor, glory, and power be to Jesus!

18. (a) The first angel announces that the judgment has come and calls upon all creation to worship God. (b) The second angel announces that Babylon (representing Rome and all human powers that oppose God's kingdom) and all its satellites have been overthrown. (c) The third angel announces that all who worship the beast (earthly powers that serve Satan) or bear the mark of the beast (showing that they belong to Satan, not to God) will suffer God's punishment with Satan in hell.

19. The godly deeds of believers testify to their faith in Jesus as their Redeemer.

Day 5 • Revelation 14:14–20

20. Both Matthew 13:24–30 and Revelation 14:14–20 speak of the judgment that will be executed at the end of the world. Both of them tell us that there will be a difference in the judgment: unbelievers (tares) and believers (wheat). It will be an occasion of great joy for the latter but a horrible experience for the former.

21. It is interesting to note that the special duty to reap the righteous is reserved for Jesus Christ (14:14–16, "seated on [a white] cloud," "with a golden crown on His head," and "a sharp sickle in His hand." How comforting that the harvest of the righteous is personally performed by Christ Himself!

22. The second harvest is the judgment of the rest of humankind, who had not believed the Gospel and trusted in Jesus as their Savior. They experience God's eternal wrath with Satan and the evil angels.

23. This city is the heavenly Jerusalem. Unbelievers will not be permitted into heaven but will experience God's wrath in hell, outside of heaven.

24. *For personal reflection. Sharing optional.* If time permits, let volunteers comment on their meditation.

Praise for God and Armageddon for the World

Revelation 15–16

Preparing for the Session

Central Focus

This week we see that the world stands under God's curse because of its rebellion against Him; but for God's people even the worst of events can bring a blessing. God is always in control. Even in the midst of persecution and tribulation He will cause blessings to result, and thus He deserves our constant praise. The people of the world fail to realize this and will suffer judgment and destruction.

Objectives

That participants, led by the Holy Spirit, will

1. see the reality of God's judgment upon the world;
2. rejoice in the victory that Christ has won over the world; and
3. praise God for revealing that victory to His own.

For the Small-Group Leader

Small-Group Discussion Helps

Day 1 • Revelation 15:1–4

1. *For personal reflection. Sharing optional.* As time permits, let volunteers comment on this "at home" meditation. Of ourselves and our own strength we are not able to withstand the devil and those powers allied with him. But God equips and provides us with powerful armor and weapons that may successfully ward off and overcome these attacks. Paul refers to this armory in terms of the protective gear and offensive weapons issued to a Roman soldier: the belt of truth, the breastplate of righteousness, shoes of the readiness given by the Gospel of peace, the shield of faith, the helmet of salvation, and the sword of the Spirit—the Word of God.

2. (a) In Exodus 15:1–18 Moses sings of how the Lord had delivered the Israelites from the pursuing Egyptians by leading the Israelites through the sea on dry land and then drowning the Egyptians. He stresses that it was the Lord's power that had accomplished this, despite the boasts of the Egyptians. This mighty deliverance would cause all people to be in awe of the Lord, who would establish the Israelites in the land He had prepared for them. (b) Moses' second song is his farewell song to the Israelites. He praises God for His mighty, saving deeds. God had carried them through the desert, caring and providing for them. The Israelites nevertheless rebelled against the Lord, and He responded by punishing them, but then He relented and had mercy on them after all. So the Lord shows Himself to be a God of mercy, as well as of justice.

3. The song in Revelation 15:3–4 also strikes the themes of God's great and marvelous deeds that cause peoples to glorify and fear Him, to acknowledge Him alone as holy and to worship Him.

Day 2 • Revelation 15:5–8

4. That the angels come out of the temple of God shows that they were doing His bidding and carrying out a mission that He had given to them. The angels are robed as Old Testament priests. This indicates that they are serving the Lord in a priestly way as they bring His judgment upon the earth.

5. (a) God's judgment on the sin committed by Adam and Eve was carried out through nature, which no longer yielded its fruit to Adam easily or without hardship and frustration. (b) Paul says that nature was caused to serve God's judgment upon sin. He hints that this natural world also will have a part in God's new creation of the age to come, that this natural world will come to share in "the freedom of the glory of the children of God."

6. (a) Not even Moses or the priests of the Old Testament were permitted to enter the temple when it was filled with God's glory since they were sinners who came from a sinful people. (b) This situation will change in the new age, when we will be forever free of sin and will share in God's glory.

Day 3 • Revelation 16:1–7

7. (a) The first bowl of wrath results in painful sores on those who had the mark of the beast (belonged to the satanic powers of this world) and worshiped his image (engaged in idolatry, worshiping the powers of this world). The sixth plague upon Egypt afflicted the Egyptians with painful boils. (b) The second and third bowls of wrath change the water of the sea, the springs, and the rivers to blood. The first plague upon Egypt changed all of the water of that country to blood.

8. (a) The angel remarks that the punishment of blood was appropriate since those whom it afflicted had shed the blood of God's people. (b) Knowing that God Himself will one day avenge His people will give persecuted Christians patience. In fact, Christians are called upon even to treat their persecutors kindly. (c) God gives persecutors time to repent and to turn to Christ. Christ has already atoned for those sins on His cross. Paul himself was a repentant persecutor of God's people. (d) *For personal reflection. Sharing optional.* Unless someone volunteers, move on to the next question. Someone *may*, of course, solicit prayers of the group for themselves and the person they seek to touch with the Gospel. In that case, pray now as a group—or reserve the prayer for the end of the session.

9. In an earlier vision the souls of Christians who had been killed for Christ's sake were associated with the altar before God's temple since they had been offered as a sacrifice.

Day 4 • Revelation 16:8–15

10. (a) Those who were afflicted with the plagues resulting from the bowls of God's wrath might have repented and turned to God for mercy. (b) Instead, they cursed God. (c) Repentance and turning to God for mercy results from faith that is given by the Holy Spirit through the Gospel. Those who refuse to hear and believe the Gospel cannot repent or turn to God for mercy. They can only despair or curse God in their misery.

11. (a) The frog-like demons released by the sixth bowl of wrath are intent on inciting the powers of this world to launch an all-out attack on God and His kingdom. (b) As time permits, share responses and insights. Jesus warns of the vicious attack of the evil powers of this world and that even some believers will turn away from the faith. However, He promises that those who stand firm to the end will be saved.

Day 5 • Revelation 16:16–21

12. On Mount Carmel the prophet Elijah challenged the prophets of Baal to engage in a contest that would prove whether the Lord or Baal is God. The losers of this contest not only were shown to be false prophets but lost their lives as well. The great final spiritual battle that is called Armageddon in Revelation 16 also masses armies of spiritual enemies against God in a great contest. This contest, too, which represents the final overthrow of evil by God when Christ comes again in His glorious power, will prove who is stronger and the real power in this world. But, as in that earlier contest, this is no contest at all, for the Lord easily and completely routs His opponents, who lose their lives—their eternal lives.

13. God's final judgment against the combined evil forces on the Last Day is seen in the lightning, thunder, hailstones, and earthquake—all signs of God's majestic glory and judgment.

14. While Christians are persecuted by and suffer from unbelievers, God's judgment does not fall upon Christians. Even when God afflicts His people, this affliction is meant only as discipline and refining, never for the purpose of punishment or destruction. For Christ has borne our punishment for us when He stood in our place under God's wrath on the cross.

15. The terrifying judgments of God revealed in this vision are not to strike Christians with terror but with the encouraging knowledge that the end of this age is coming soon and that the time when we will live forever with God in glory is fast approaching.

The Agony of the Wicked and the Ecstasy of the Saved

Revelation 17–19

Preparing for the Session

Central Focus

Satan seduces the people of this world, luring them into idolatry and service to him in his goal of destroying the church. But God shows us that these seductive powers will be destroyed along with the Antichrist's power and propaganda. God's people will triumph victoriously and celebrate joyously their marriage to the Lamb.

Objectives

That participants, led by the Holy Spirit, will

1. realize that Satan's efforts to seduce the world are doomed to destruction, as are his Antichrist power and propaganda;
2. rejoice to see Christ preserve His own, while Satan and his helpers are destroyed; and
3. see the seductive ungodliness of this world slain by Him who sat upon the white horse and now is crowned King of kings and Lord of lords.

For the Small-Group Leader

Since the Book of Revelation is not an easily discernible story, it is advisable for the small-group discussion leader regularly to call attention to the golden thread tying the entire book together: "Jesus Christ is King of kings and Lord of lords forever!" The most effective way to do this is to review the theme of each week's study and tie it to the preceding and succeeding ones and show the continuity and the progress. Sessions 1 and 2 introduce Jesus Christ as Lord of the church and of the world. In session 3 we saw how Jesus led His own through trouble to triumph. Session 4 showed us that God would shake up the world but keep the church safe and secure. Then in sessions 5 and 6 God exposed the enemies of the church and promised that Christ would gain the victory. Such a brief review will prepare the members of the class for the three last sessions, which announce the agony and doom of all the wicked and the eternal victory for all the disciples of Jesus Christ.

Small-Group Discussion Helps

Day 1 • Revelation 17

1. Participants will probably easily see why the Bible likens idolatry to spiritual adultery. Just as in adultery a spouse takes a love that belongs only to his or her mate and gives it to another, so in idolatry someone takes worship and trust that belong only to God and gives them to another being. In Old Testament times idolatry often did involve actual adultery as well, since some heathen religions (including religions in Old Testament Canaan and New Testament Greece) involved sex with a shrine prostitute as a means of contact with the god.

2. (a) Revelation 17:4 describes the seductiveness of the prostitute in John's vision by describing her as clothed in fine, beautiful garments, wearing dazzling gems, and holding a cup containing an intoxicating beverage. Certainly sin finds many ways to be appealing to people in our own age, promising pleasure and power. In our own sex-charged age, idolatry (as in ancient times) is frequently coupled with sex. (b) *For personal reflection. Sharing optional.* Do not ask for responses to this exercise. You may want to comment that in John's vision the prostitute's clients are said to be drunk with the wine of her adulteries. The appeal of sin dulls our thinking and lulls us into a false sense of well-being, disguising or hiding the consequences that inevitably result from sin. James describes the downward course of sin when he writes: "each person is tempted when he is lured and enticed by his own desire. Then desire when it has conceived gives birth to sin, and sin when it is full-grown brings forth death" (James 1:14–15). In the Lord's Prayer, we ask God to "lead us not into temptation"—to guard and keep us and to give us strength to overcome temptation.

3. The prostitute's goals are right in line with those of Satan, her master and lord: to make war against Christ in this world by bringing down His church. But in this, Satan and his allies will not succeed; the victory already belongs to Christ, a victory in which the church shares.

4. While rulers today rarely insist on being worshiped as gods, governments in our era have attempted to forbid people to believe in or worship God or spread His kingdom and have taught and commanded people to lie and kill to further those governments' goals.

5. As time permits, let people share examples from their experience. In Bible history we have such notable examples as the Roman emperor calling for a worldwide census—to fulfill prophecy as Mary and Joseph thereby move to Bethlehem, where the Savior is to be born. Another example: God turning the wickedness of Joseph's brothers to good, "to bring it about that many people should be kept alive" (Genesis 50:20).

Day 2 • Revelation 18:1–20

6. (a) Moses' face was radiant when he came down from Mount Sinai because he had come from the presence of the Lord. The angel's splendor may well also indicate that he comes from the Lord's presence and represents the Lord in pronouncing judgment upon the prostitute. (b) As time permits, share responses.

7. (a) Answers, of course, may legitimately vary. But a sweet and gentle Gospel tone surely is inherent in the phrase "*my* people" and in the plea not to "share in her plagues." (b) We must always be aware of the deceptions put forth by Satan.

8. (a) The kings of the earth (those who ally themselves with ungodliness to gain personal power over others), the merchants of the earth (those who ally themselves with ungodliness to gain financially), and the seamen who transport the merchants' goods (those who profit by assisting others in their evil) will share in the punishment that is to come upon the seductive ungodliness of this world. (b) These three types of collaborators still make alliances with ungodliness and evil to advance their own power and pleasure in this world. Those who rule over others using unfair tactics may be found on nearly every level of relationships, from families and places of employment to organizations of all kinds to government on every level. Those who gain financially from others by using dishonesty or unfair leverage may also be found in many businesses, professions, and industries.

9. When people try to get ahead in this world by ungodly means and do not repent, what they have gained will one day vanish and not return. Ruin will be eternal, as they share in the fall of Satan and his kingdom.

10. *For personal reflection. Sharing optional.* Move to the next question.

Day 3 • Revelation 18:21–19:10

11. Jesus, in describing His sudden, surprising second coming into this world as Judge at the end of the age, compares it to the destruction that fell on the world in the time of Noah, when the deluge drowned all unbelievers, and to the rain of fire and sulfur that came upon Sodom after the Lord called Lot and his family to leave that city. Like Revelation 18:22–23, Jesus speaks of how the ordinary, ongoing activities of life will meet a sudden and unexpected end. Music, daily work, evenings at home, weddings, merchandising—all will suddenly cease, to the complete surprise of unbelievers, who will be overwhelmed. (Believers, however, have been forewarned so that that day need not catch them unaware.)

12. Two sins of the ungodly world are underlined in this account of the sudden coming of judgment—leading people into sin to their eternal destruction and murdering prophets, believers, and other victims.

13. The punishment of the wicked and unbelieving will be eternal in its duration. The devils and lost souls in hell will also live forever, but in the misery of hell. As they rejected the Lord in this life, so they will be apart from the Lord forever, as Revelation 19:3b and Mark 9:43–48 indicate. This realization surely will move us to redouble our prayers and witness to unbelieving relatives, friends, and acquaintances and our support of world evangelization through our church.

14. (a) The church (believers) is called Christ's bride. This picture tells us much about our relationship to Jesus, His love for us, our nearness to Him, our covenant relationship with Him, and the faithfulness we are called upon to show to Him. (b) Isaiah 61:10 speaks of how the Lord has "clothed" and "covered" the believer in bridal finery. The righteousness produced in the Christian is the work of God within us and is also a result of His grace. God rewards and commends Christians for what He Himself has done in them! (c) The church is invited to a marriage feast. This feast represents that Christians will begin living with Christ in an eternal communion in the kingdom of heaven. (In the Bible, a wedding feast was celebrated when a bridegroom took his bride to their own home and began living with her.)

15. *For personal reflection. Sharing optional.* Encourage participants to share their feelings about God's invita-

tion to them personally to join in Christ's victory celebration in heaven.

Day 4 • Revelation 19:11–16

16. **Challenge question.** (a) The horse's rider is called "Faithful and True"—Jesus speaks of Himself in the letter to Laodicea as the "Amen, the faithful and true witness. (b) The rider's eyes are "like a flame of fire"; Jesus reveals Himself initially to John as one whose eyes are "like a flame of fire." The same characteristic is referred to in the letter to Thyatira. (c) The name of the rider is "the Word of God"; in his Gospel, John refers to Jesus as the Word that was made flesh. (d) Out of the rider's mouth comes a sharp sword. In the first vision of Revelation Jesus is seen as having a sharp, double-edged sword coming from His mouth, a characteristic repeated in the letter to Pergamum. (e) On the rider's thigh is written the name "King of kings and Lord of lords"; Paul refers to God with this phrase in his first letter to Timothy. In Genesis 32:25–30, God touched Jacob's *thigh* ("hip socket"), when, in the form of an ordinary man, He wrestled with Jacob. Then God blessed Jacob and gave him the name *Israel*. (*Israel* means "he struggles with God.") Thus the name written on the "thigh" of the Lord Christ indicates that the real conqueror of God—the one who successfully endured the judgment of God the Father—is Jesus Christ, Son of the Father and descendant of the patriarch Israel.

17. What a comfort to know that our Lord Jesus, the one to whom we belong, the one who loves us so much as to die for us—this Jesus rules the powers of this world, even those that do not acknowledge Him. Even so, they are in His control. Encourage participants to say what this means to them personally.

Day 5 • Revelation 19:17–21

18. Whereas the marriage supper of the Lamb is a victory celebration in which believers join their Lord in enjoying His victory of the forces of evil that were opposed to Him, the "great supper of God" refers to the grisly meal that carrion-eating birds enjoy as they devour the dead bodies of God's defeated foes. The picture is one that comes from ancient times when the bodies of killed soldiers lay on battlefields and were eaten by vultures, a military roadkill. The first feast results from victory; the second results from defeat.

19. While the Lord's protecting hand will not let any power, not even the devil himself, snatch us away from Him, we Christians may give in to the lures and wiles of the devil and his allies so that we, willingly and of our own choice, lose our place in God's kingdom and pass away with Satan, the demons, and the ungodly world around us. This danger is very real, and the Holy Spirit earnestly warns us about it repeatedly in the Bible. Demas was one who deserted the kingdom of God and joined the ungodly world, but there are many like him.

20. The Holy Spirit encourages us by telling us that God will keep us safe, that while the world is under the control of Satan, we belong to Christ, who is the true God and eternal life. The tragedy that will overtake the ungodly world will not overtake believers.

The Millennium and the Doom of Satan

Revelation 20

Preparing for the Session

Central Focus

In this cycle we see Satan bound for a thousand years (the millennium), during which time he will be restricted in his opposition to Christ and in his persecution of the church. Then for a final time, after the millennium, Satan will be granted opportunity for a brief period of most harsh persecution before he is cast "into the lake of fire" forever.

Objectives

That participants, led by the Holy Spirit, will

1. gain a correct understanding of the millennium;
2. grow in conviction of God's grace in Christ providing for eternal salvation; and
3. help fellow Christians focus their attention on the final victory of Christ and on the defeat of Satan and his followers.

For the Small-Group Leader

Since so many Christians have been exposed to nonscriptural views concerning the millennium, the small-group discussion leader will pray and prepare diligently that this Study 8, with its emphasis on the millennium, will not disturb the fine Christian fellowship that has developed in these sessions. Accordingly, we make the following suggestions: (a) Fit this Study 8 into the total context of the Book of Revelation, whose theme is the victorious Christ, who is in constant combat with evil people and powers and overcomes them all. The chief opponent is the devil, whom Christ restricts for "a thousand years" (a millennium) in his satanic plans to overthrow the church. (b) Various theories and publications have caused much confusion about the millennium. The small-group discussion leader should urge frankness but also patience in allowing all to discuss questions freely.

Small-Group Discussion Helps

Day 1 • Revelation 20:1–3

1. Jesus, because He has overcome death and Satan by His death and resurrection, holds the keys of death and Hades. Some commentators consequently believe that the "angel" in Revelation 20:1 is Christ Himself (though this would be the only time in Revelation where Christ would be called an angel) or that perhaps the angel acts as Christ's agent.

2. This binding and confining took place when Jesus overcame the devil during His ministry on earth, climaxing with His suffering and death on the cross. Following His death Jesus "went and proclaimed to the spirits in prison [Hades]" (1 Peter 3:19) to proclaim His victory over Satan and Hades. His resurrection demonstrated His victory over death.

3. (a) Jesus briefly outlines the events that will take place from His ascension to the end of the age when He will come again in His glory. These events include the appearance of false saviors; wars, rumors of wars, and conflicts among nations; famines, earthquakes, and other natural disasters; persecution and hatred of Christians; falling away from faith by some Christians, disputes and conflicts among those who identify themselves as Christians, and apathy within the church; and, through it all, the proclamation of the Gospel throughout the world.

4. Despite the power of Satan's forces mounted against Christians, (a) the forces of hell will not be able to prevail over the church, (b) nor will individual Christians be snatched away from Christ against their will.

5. At the end of this age ("immediately"), Jesus will come visibly and gloriously, bringing an end to this present age and world. Everyone will see His coming—believers with joy, unbelievers with terror and distress. All people will then be gathered for the judgment. Believers will be invited to an eternity of joy in heaven, and unbelievers will be sent to an eternity of punishment in hell.

Day 2 • Revelation 20:4

6. The fact that John sees the "souls" of the martyrs indicates that he is looking into heaven before the resurrection at the Last Day, while the bodies of these faithful witnesses were still in their graves on earth.

7. (a) Paul tells us that those who die with Christ and endure with Him will also live and reign with Him, corresponding to the "thrones" and those "seated on them," who "came to life and reigned with Christ." (b) "Do you not know that the saints will judge the world?" Paul asks, corresponding to "those to whom the authority to judge was committed." God will cause His saints—those whom He has made holy through Jesus—to share in His glory. (c) Jesus calls "blessed" those who are persecuted and slandered, like the prophets, for their reward will be "great in heaven," corresponding to "those who had been beheaded for the testimony of Jesus for the word of God."

8. Jesus says that someone who believes in Him has "passed from death to life." John says that those who believe "have life in His name." These passages and others speak of coming to faith (conversion) as a coming to life from the dead.

9. This verse is encouraging to us as it tells us of faithful believers who already live and reign with Christ even before the resurrection at the end of time! This verse is particularly comforting when we think of those who have suffered for Jesus' sake while on this earth. Encourage participants to share their own comments indicating why they find verse 4 comforting and encouraging.

Day 3 • Revelation 20:5–6

10. When Jesus comes again in His glory at the Last Day, their bodies will be raised. They will then recognize and acknowledge Him as the Lord. However, this awakening will then be too late to save them.

11. Coming to faith is referred to in Scripture as a resurrection from the dead, since those who do not have a relationship of faith with Christ are dead to God, as unable to respond to Him as a corpse is unable to respond to those around it. But God, by the power of the Gospel, brings people to life so that they are able to respond to Him and have a loving relationship with Him when they come to faith in Him. Paul connects this resurrection to the power of the Gospel that is in Baptism. (a) The first death, which all humanity experiences (except those who are still alive when Christ comes again [1 Thessalonians 4:15]) is the death of the body, when the soul leaves it and goes either to heaven to be with Christ until the resurrection at the end of the age or to wait in Hades (hell) for Judgment Day. (b) The second death, which only unbelievers will experience, is to be sent to hell to spend eternity forever separated from the love and grace of God.

12. Hell, the second death, has no power over believers because Christ has freed us from punishment in hell by being punished for our sins on the cross. All of our sins have been laid on Jesus, who has paid the full and complete penalty for all of our sins. No punishment, therefore, is due us, thanks to Jesus.

13. Rather than being something to dread or fear, death for believers will be the entrance into an eternity in glory, where we will live with Christ, our Savior, sharing in His eternal joy and peace. Paul called this "far better" than life on this earth, no matter how good we might find our life here.

Day 4 • Revelation 20:7–10

14. (a) In both Revelation 20:9 and Ezekiel 38:22, God Himself defeats Gog by sending down fire from heaven to devour the army gathered against God's people. This figurative statement emphasizes that God Himself will overcome the onslaught of the enemies of His church and bring them to judgment. (b) *For personal reflection. Sharing optional.* God Himself fights for His people and defeats their enemies. We find our refuge, our protecting fortress, in Him. All we have to do is trust in God and rest quietly in the confidence that the Lord will protect us and put our enemies to rout.

15. While the devil, his allies, and his followers are real and should be taken seriously (1 Peter 5:8–9) and guarded against, God's grace will not allow them to separate us from Him or to deprive us of the joy and peace of His kingdom, either in this world or the next. Nothing—absolutely nothing—is able to come between us and the love of God, now or ever. Encourage participants to share their own statements of confidence about this.

Day 5 • Revelation 20:11–15

16. All people who have ever lived, from Adam and Eve to the last generation on this earth, will stand before God to be judged. This includes believers as well as unbelievers.

17. (a) The "books" contain the complete record of the life of every person who has ever lived. (b) On the basis of such a record, no person should expect to be declared innocent, for all who have ever lived (except Jesus Himself) have sinned against God continuously and grievously. Such a record would condemn any and all of us. (c) But God has blotted out sins from the record of believers for the sake of Christ, who has atoned, paid the penalty, for all these sins so that they might be expunged from the record. When God examines the life of a believer, He looks at that record through Christ and finds nothing to condemn, since He sees only the righteousness of Jesus with which we are clothed, covering our sins completely.

18. The Book of Life contains the names of believers, who have been saved through faith in the redeeming work of Christ. These names have been written into the Book of Life because of the grace of God, His unmerited love and favor, not because of merit or worthiness on our part. Having our names written in the Book of Life is another way of saying that we are saved, which is by the grace of God.

19. We are saved solely by God's grace—His undeserved favor and His forgiveness He gives us because of the perfect life and the suffering, death, and resurrection of Jesus, who thereby paid the penalty for our sins and endured the eternal punishment we deserve. *Having* been saved, God now by His Spirit encourages and leads us to do good works *as a response* to His love. We do "good works" (i.e., show love to God and to people) not *in order to be* saved but because we *are* saved! Note that the judgment on the Last Day actually takes place *before* any mention of works. Jesus separates the sheep from the goats. On what basis? Faith or unbelief. But because faith cannot be seen, the visible works are pointed to as *evidence* of the faith or nonfaith of the judged persons. Note that the critical element in the good works or their lack is whether the person did them "for Christ," recognizing or refusing to recognize "brothers," who are brothers and sisters of Jesus through their faith in Him (Galatians 3:26).

20. Paul calls death the "last enemy" of God's people to be destroyed, which corresponds to what we are told in Revelation 20:14.

Our Victorious Lord Reigns Forever

Revelation 21–22

Preparing for the Session

Central Focus

The purpose of God's action on our behalf in history is to bring us back to where He intended us to be in the beginning—in complete fellowship with God in bliss and perfection. We joyfully anticipate the coming of our Lord to bring to completion all He has begun.

Objectives

That participants, led by the Holy Spirit, will

1. appreciate the problems of interpreting apocalyptic writing, but at the same time rejoice in the central message of Christ's certain victory over Satan for all eternity;
2. look joyfully for the return of our Lord and recognize the importance of being prepared at all times for His return; and
3. be encouraged to continue to read and study the Book of Revelation personally and in fellowship with other believers for comfort and encouragement in Christian faith and life.

For the Small-Group Leader

Congratulations! Any leader of a group studying the Book of Revelation deserves appreciative response. Simply to launch forth upon such a study requires courage and faith, and then to keep a group together until the course is completed calls forth even greater determination. Accept any positive evaluations, as well as constructive criticisms graciously. Continue to pray fervently and to work enthusiastically that group Bible study will grow and flourish in your congregation.

Small-Group Discussion Helps

Day 1 • Revelation 21:1–8

1. The sea here has a symbolic, not a literal meaning. (a) The sea represents a powerful, uncontrollable force that could cause death and great destruction. (b) Storms at sea were a sign of the approaching end of the age and the coming judgment. (c) The beast, the servant of Satan, arose from the sea.

2. As time permits, encourage participants to share responses. God will dwell personally among His people. Sorrow will be no more, nor will there be any cause for sorrow. Death will no longer be, nor will anyone experience any pain. The old order of suffering and disappointment, hardship and grief, will be gone, replaced by constant, enduring joy, satisfaction, peace, and well-being. All this will be different from what we now know. All this will be new.

3. A number of closely related answers are possible! The good news of the forgiveness of sins that we receive through faith in Christ wells up in our heart and overflows in joy, praise, and love for God and people. Ultimately, we find the spring of living water in Jesus Himself. He satisfies us with salvation. In the John 4 text, living water is the eternal life we receive; in the John 7 text, it's identified with the Holy Spirit, who brings us to faith through the Gospel and who lives in our hearts to keep us in faith and to lead us to grow in faith and Christian life. Note that the water is "without payment"—purely by God's grace.

4. It is not the sins themselves that keep people out of God's kingdom, either in this world or the next. Otherwise none of us would ever enter God's kingdom. But it is persisting in these sins, without repentance, that will, in the end, condemn people before God and will keep them out of God's heavenly kingdom. By God's grace in Christ all sins are forgiven—except the sin of refusing to repent and believe, for this sin (the sin against the Holy Spirit) refuses God's gracious forgiveness and persistently continues in unrepentant defiance of God.

Day 2 • Revelation 21:9–27

5. That the heavenly Jerusalem bears both the names of the 12 tribes of Old Testament Israel and the names of the 12 apostles, the foundational leaders of the New Testament church, shows that the heavenly Jerusalem includes all of God's people, whether they lived under the old covenant, awaiting the Messiah, or under the new covenant, trusting in the Lord who died and rose for them.

6. The high priest's breastplate was studded with 12 precious stones: sardius, topaz, carbuncle, emerald, sapphire, diamond, jacinth, agate, amethyst, beryl, onyx, and jasper. The foundations of the heavenly city are made also of 12 precious stones: jasper, sapphire, agate, emerald, onyx, carnelian, chrysolite, beryl, topaz, chrysoprase, jacinth, and amethyst. Since the Hebrew and Greek names of these gems are often difficult to link exactly with their English equivalents, the two collections of precious stones may refer to the same gems. In any case, the similarity suggests that the heavenly Jerusalem has a holy character. Peter calls Christians, even on earth, "a royal priesthood, a holy nation, a people for His own possession" (1 Peter 2:9).

7. The cube shape of the heavenly Jerusalem corresponds to the shape of the Most Holy Place of the tabernacle or temple in the Old Testament. Just as the glory of God filled the Most Holy Place, so God Himself dwells in the heavenly Jerusalem (Revelation 21:10–11; 22:3). (The cube—a "perfect" three-dimensional structure may also be taken as a symbol of the Trinity: one God in three persons.)

8. There will be no need to close the gates of the city since all that could threaten the city or its inhabitants have been removed and confined to hell forever. There will be no need to fear the darkness, for there will be no darkness. The gates of the city will remain open to receive believers from all nations who will enter the city. As in other passages, night here represents the darkness of evil and sin. No evil or sin will be found in the city.

9. Encourage participants to tell which characteristics of the city they find most appealing. Perhaps it will be the opportunity to see Jesus face-to-face or the absence of any trouble or grief.

Day 3 • Revelation 22:1–5

10. Comparing the Garden of Eden (Genesis 2:8–14) to the new Jerusalem (Revelation 22:1–5), we note some striking similarities. In Eden there was a river to water the garden and there were trees "pleasant to the sight and good for food." There were two special trees: the tree of life and the tree of the knowledge of good and evil. All in the Garden of Eden was perfect, created for the praise of God and the enjoyment of God's people forever. For the new heaven and the new earth the angel showed John a river also, "bright as crystal, flowing from the throne of God and of the Lamb through the middle of the street of the city." It will be "the water of life." There will also be the tree of life with its 12 kinds of fruit, yielding its fruit every month. Even the leaves will serve "for the healing of the nations." There will be nothing accursed, and all will be praising God. All will have the blessed privilege to see God's face and to identify with God personally, for "His name will be on their foreheads." God will be all in all to them. In Him they will have all light and all rights, for "they will reign forever and ever."

11. The river of the water of life flows from the throne of God the Father and of the Lamb (Jesus, God the Son). In John 7 Jesus identifies the streams of living water with the Holy Spirit.

12. (a) The curse that hangs over people now is their inability to keep the Law; this puts them under God's punishment for falling short of His will. (b) Jesus Christ redeemed us from the curse by perfectly keeping the Law for us (His "active obedience") and by assuming our guilt and making atonement for us when He suffered and died on the cross (His "passive obedience").

13. (a) The fact that those in the heavenly city see the face of God shows that all sin has been removed from them, for no sinner—not even Moses, the servant of God—is able to see the face of God and live. (b) God's name on the foreheads of those within the city shows that they belong to God and are under His protection and blessing.

14. Encourage participants to share their thoughts on what it will be like to reign with God. Since all believers will reign with God, this surely does not mean that we will dominate one another. Perhaps reigning with God will mean that we will meet with no obstacles or limitations to our wishes or desires (which will be fully in line with God's own wishes and desires). In the new heaven and *new earth* (2 Peter 3:13) in which we shall live, we will be able to exercise dominion over a new, redeemed creation (Romans 8:19–22), fulfilling God's original intent that was frustrated when our first parents sinned and brought catastrophe not only on themselves but on all creation (Genesis 3:17).

Day 4 • Revelation 22:6–11

15. In Revelation 1:1 John states the purpose of the book as "to show to His servants the things that must soon take place." In 22:6 the angel says he was sent "to show His servants what must soon take place." The past tense indicates that this purpose has been completed.

16. (a) The central message is Jesus' affirmation, repeated three times: "I am coming soon." (b) This is a message of warning to unbelievers and those who oppose God's kingdom, and it is a message of comfort to God's long-suffering people.

17. (a) With the Book of Revelation the Holy Spirit completed the inspiration of the Bible. God has now given His complete Word to the world, and He has commissioned His church to proclaim that Word to all the world. The Holy Spirit works through that Word to enable people to believe it. God has done everything possible to bring His saving Word to people; if people do not now receive it as His Word, believe it, and live according to it, the responsibility for the resulting condemnation and loss rests with those who refused God's Word. If sinners are lost after hearing God's Word, it is their own fault. (b) The implications for us to whom the Word is addressed are clear: We are to receive the Word as the Word of God to us, trust its message, and live according to its precepts. (c) The implications for us who are called to speak God's Word to others are also clear: Our responsibility is to communicate God's Word clearly, so it may be understood. We are not responsible for how that clearly communicated Word is received.

Day 5 • Revelation 22:12–21

18. (a) **Challenge question.** To wash our robes means to look to Jesus in repentance and faith for forgiveness and cleansing, since He has atoned for our sins by His sacrificial death on the cross. (b) Both phrases in rich imagery tell us that we'll live forever, with Jesus, in His kingdom of glory.

19. (a) The Holy Spirit and the bride (the church) keep inviting sinners to come and satisfy their thirst for eternal life with God. We, God's people, issue this invitation by proclaiming the Gospel and urging sinners to repent and to believe the Good News of redemption offered to them through faith in Jesus, the Savior. (b) Encourage participants to speak of the ways in which they personally and together with other Christians through their church are sharing the Gospel with others and inviting them into God's kingdom.

20. God's Word is the offer of salvation through faith in Jesus alone. Since there is only one Savior and one Gospel, we must take care to see that we pass along this Gospel purely and without adding human opinions to it or subtracting any of God's truth from it. God's Word of the Gospel offers the only way that people may be saved, so it is crucial that it be communicated clearly and correctly.

21. Encourage participants to share benefits they have received from the Book of Revelation. Close the discussion session by offering a prayer thanking God for the opportunity to study this part of God's Word together.